WINNING IN
A MAN'S WORLD

WINNING IN A MAN'S WORLD

Advice for Women Who Want to Succeed

and the Men Who Work with Them

Renee Weisman

To order additional copies of this book, contact:
Xlibris Corporation
1-888-795-4274
www.Xlibris.com
Orders@Xlibris.com
51741

Contents

Contents

Dedication

In memory of the woman who showed me you can work full time, have a happy marriage and a loving family, and keep your priorities straight: my mother, Clare Kronberg.

Acknowledgments

This book grew from numerous discussions I had with my daughters (and their friends) about their careers and the many employees, male and female, that I mentored during my career. Carin constantly encouraged me to "write it all down," and when I did, helped me edit and improve each section. Stacy gave me helpful ideas and cheered me every step of the way. They, along with two great sons-in-law, gave me three of the most delightful grandchildren, Alyza, Carly, and Maxwell. My husband John always pushed me to achieve more—and to ask for more as well. You are my best cheerleader. A special thanks to Norman Cherbino, Jim Keller, and the staff at Langton Cherbino Group for the wonderful cover graphics. Thanks also to Evelyn Menina, Lindsea Therese Tacadong, and Dawny June Ebite for copy editing and to Carin Crook for text editing. Sherwin Soy and Kathleen Zulueta provided excellent design and formatting suggestions and were very patient with my many questions. Melvin Frost and Sarah Arizala kept the entire publishing process moving. Finally, I want to acknowledge the many wonderful people I worked with and for at IBM.

Foreword

Men and women think and behave differently. As a result, many career women working in a largely male environment find it hard to get their ideas implemented, to move at the same rate as their male counterparts, and to find a balance between their home and work commitments. In many cases, these women may even leave the business rather than deal with the fundamental issues. At the same time, men who work for and with women, sell to women, or otherwise interact with them can become much more effective by understanding certain fundamental issues. This book is designed to share my experiences in a largely male environment in the hope that both sexes can benefit from what I learned.

Why do you really need another book on men and women at work? Most self-help books tell you what to do but not *how* to do it. And those that do explain how are, frankly, dull. This book is extremely tactical, giving you step-by-step instructions with real examples and lessons learned. Each chapter includes specific worksheets ("Try It Now") and special advice ("Renee's Rules") to help you apply the principles and get comfortable with them. Read the chapter, do the exercises, try the results, and redo and revisit the exercises periodically.

I joined IBM in 1969, a lone-woman engineer hired into an engineering group of over 400 men. In those days, it was a common occurrence for other male engineers to stop by my desk to ask me to type something since they assumed I must be a secretary. In 2003, I achieved the title of Distinguished Engineer in IBM, a position at that time held by less than 250 men and a dozen women worldwide. I have also managed several thousand employees in multiple engineering and technical organizations, largely male. I have worked and succeeded in a man's world; but it did not come without a considerable amount of learning, adapting, and, above all, humor. I also did it without a full-time nanny or live-in help.

Most successful women say, "If I only knew then what I know now." My hope is that this book will help women learn these secrets earlier in their careers so they can overcome the inherent traits that have held them back. And as a male managing, mentoring, or working for women in your organization or as clients, this book will open your eyes to differences you may never have considered.

Who I Am and Why I Wrote This Book

My name is Renee Weisman. Until I retired in 2008, I was a Distinguished Engineer and a Director of Engineering at International Business Machines Corporation (IBM) with a total of thirty-nine years in industry and education. I was also a working mother and now a grandmother. I was the only woman engineer in many areas for almost ten years and one of the first woman engineering managers in my division.

I first joined IBM in 1969, three weeks after graduating college and two weeks after getting married! Three months later, I became pregnant with my first child and started working toward my master's degree.

When my daughter was born, I took a three-month (unpaid) maternity leave and a nine-month (unpaid) educational leave, expecting to return at the end of the year. During that year, I did considerable substitute teaching at local high schools and colleges and found to my surprise that I liked to teach. Since at that time there were no practical IBM part-time work options for my position, I decided to resign from IBM after the year's leave expired.

I taught for ten years, teaching about fifteen to twenty hours per week with probably an equivalent amount of prep time outside of class. This flexible schedule worked well for me through the birth of my second child four years later and until both girls were in school. I returned to IBM full-time when my daughters were five and nine— eleven years after originally joining the firm.

I felt compelled to write this book after taking an active role in mentoring women in technology, sponsoring network groups, and being told again and again that I should write down this advice. Hearing my stories often helped others realize that their issues were not unique. Surprisingly, the men started attending my sessions as often as the women, and said I gave them a fresh perspective they had not considered.

This is not a "cookbook" or a "playbook," but the methods and experiences are designed to help you rethink your situation. The "Try It Now" exercises are on topics that I wish someone had shown me along the way. So whether you are male or female, a manager or an employee, a new hire or an experienced worker, this book can help you.

I had the benefit of working in a company where all people were valued, and diversity was encouraged. What this book teaches is even more important if you are in a less-enlightened company.

1

Trial by Fire: Being the Only Woman in a Man's World

Whenever you are asked if you can do a job, tell 'em,
"Certainly, I can!" Then get busy and find out how to do it.
—Teddy Roosevelt

Your career begins your very first day at work. First impressions are made immediately, and the behavioral habits you practice early in your career can help set the stage for future success. So why do so many people say, "If I could do it all over, I'd . . . ?" You can't prevent making mistakes, but you can definitely learn from the ones others make instead of repeating them yourselves.

That being said, I know very few people who started their first job loving it. College may teach you what you need to know technically, but it does not prepare you for the business and political agendas you will encounter. My first day after returning to industry from teaching was so frustrating, I almost quit! Today I laugh about that experience, but at the time, I was shocked. About twenty-five people (twenty-three of them men) joined the company that day. After we filled out the necessary forms and went over basic orientation items, our managers were supposed to pick us up and take us to our new work locations. As manager after manager arrived, the new employees filed out of the conference room. After about an hour, everyone had left except the new hire coordinator and me. This coordinator stepped out to place some frantic phone calls. Shortly thereafter, I heard my new manager's

15

name being paged over the PA system (remember, this preceded cell phones). Another hour passed, and my manager finally arrived to pick me up.

Okay, I thought, *maybe we're off to a bad start but it'll get better.*

I then followed my manager by car to the building in which I'd be working. (They all looked alike). Once we arrived, he informed me that neither my desk nor my office were ready. There were no extra offices, but someone was leaving in three weeks, so until then I could use the desks of people on vacation. Since no single person was on vacation, this meant I would need to move from desk to desk and office to office each day. Of course, I had no key or place to put my personal belongings. (He never considered that a woman would want to lock up a purse.)

By then it was lunchtime, and we went to the cafeteria for my first IBM lunch. We sat with other members of the department, all male. After a quick introduction, the conversation quickly steered to fishing and football.

After lunch, my manager introduced me to the engineer who was supposed to "train" me. This individual also had been recently hired but had more than twenty-five years of experience and described himself as a technical expert in the area. Unfortunately, this trainer had absolutely no idea what my job was and proceeded to talk at length about himself. When I asked questions about the specific process to which we were supposed to provide engineering support, he expounded at length about the chemistry of the process. Now I was new to industry, but I had an advanced degree in chemistry. Listening to this individual, I could not help but doubt he understood anything about science.

Finally, the day ended, and I went to find my car. Of course, since no one had really shown me around the place, it took me three tries and twenty minutes (it was a big building) before I found the right exit door to the parking lot.

When I arrived home, my husband was excitedly waiting in the driveway to hear all about my first day. I got out of the car and said, "If I have one more day like this one was, I am going back to teaching."

Needless to say, I didn't return to teaching, and the next day was much better. There had been a major yield problem the prior weekend.

The line was put under engineering control, and I was asked to work twelve-hour shifts on my second day of work! All of the engineers were asked to be out on the line to bring things back to normal. I learned more in the next few days than I would have learned in a month under normal circumstances. We took tools apart and put them back together; we dumped chemical baths and remade them; and with all of the engineers around, I asked a lot of questions.

One week later, a task force was formed to "fix" the yield problems. By this time, I knew so much about the tools and processes that people were coming to me for answers! Needless to say, we applied good scientific principles, some experiments to test them out, and extensive data analyses to ensure we weren't missing anything. As a result, the line had the best performance ever. I watched the task force leader and learned that there is absolutely *no* substitute for data. This is a major lesson for any discipline. You can draw anything on paper, model something with the very best of models, but success is about getting the right data, interpreting it properly, and taking appropriate action. A senior statistician took me under his wing and showed me how to run important analyses to be sure that I was interpreting the data correctly. I found this knowledge invaluable with so much data arriving every day.

I describe this introduction to my life in industry for several reasons. First, never put too much stock in your first day. I was ready to quit after day one, but day two was much better. Next, focus on the job to be done and do it well. Results matter. Finally, many people will advise you throughout your career. Just because they claim to have "experience" or have been doing it longer doesn't mean they are necessarily doing it better. You bring fresh eyes, a new perspective, a set of unique talents, and a desire to excel at the job. Use that and have the confidence in yourself to follow it through. This isn't to say that you don't want to take advice from others; just take it with a grain of salt. Get to know the depth and integrity of your coworkers so you know from whom you really should seek advice. Even though I had taken several college courses in statistics, that on-the-job applied statistics introduction has been something upon which I have relied throughout my career. Don't let the "experts" turn you away from something you believe is right.

Another important point I learned is not to be afraid of a crisis. If everything is wonderful and you join the group, the expectation is that everything will stay wonderful; therefore, any failure must be yours. But if you go to an area needing improvement and you make it better, people will credit you with that success. You also will get more notice, both positive and negative, in an area that has problems.

One of my advisors used to compare different assignments to the electric company. Since everyone expects the power to always be on, when it's out we get upset. If an area runs like the electric company, and the power stays on, it's what people expect. As such, even if your work is flawless, it is underappreciated. What's worse, if you happen to get there when the power goes out, you will be associated with the failure. If, on the other hand, you go to an area that has very poor service and you make it run like an electric company, you will get credited with the improvement. Since it obviously wasn't running well before you got there, it must have been a difficult job to fix, and even a few flaws are tolerated. Throughout my career, I always tried to go to the trouble spots. The areas with problems affecting business performance almost always get priority in analysis, hiring, spending, and support. As such, you can make a difference more quickly, and everyone pulls together to make a success happen. It's a win-win for you and for the company to go into a riskier environment, provided you can tolerate the time and the pressure. Run to the problems, not away from them.

During those early months, I faced another event where I was encouraged to do something with which I didn't agree, and I held firm. Again, we were experiencing process problems, and I had been carefully inspecting products at every step in the operation to identify where a particular defect originated. My counterpart (that same "expert trainer" from day one) came up with a process to fix a particular defect based on his "widespread knowledge." I didn't agree based on my empirical study and recommended a different alternative. Being anxious to get the process fixed quickly, everyone suggested we implement both changes at once. I insisted we do the two separately to understand the impacts of each change and even suggested my counterpart's idea go first. His change was made the next day, and the defect level actually increased!

We then removed his change, added my process recommendation, and the defect essentially disappeared.

Several recommendations for success come out of this. Number one: Know your facts and stick to the facts. Always work off data if possible. Theory is great, but data is better. Number two: Don't make two changes at the same time. Number three: It isn't necessary to be the first change, just be the right one. Having the "expert" make the issue worse and then having my fix eliminate the defect made my accomplishment that much more recognized. In fact, it led to my receiving a generous award within my first six months at work. (By the way, one thing I have experienced throughout my career is that the good people rise to the top, and the lower contributors will fall out. The "expert" never really delivered, and he was not with IBM long. As I said before and will say again, results matter.)

Other experiences in my early years show some of the changes women brought to the workplace. I had been with the company less than a month when one of the technical leaders asked me to join him at a senior manager review meeting. While I had worked on the topic, I was only casually involved in the solutions, and I really didn't know why he wanted me there. However, I thought it would be a good opportunity to see senior managers making decisions. (Remember that all the managers and engineers were male, and this was almost thirty years ago.) We walked into the smoke-filled meeting room, where several senior managers were clearly displeased with what they were seeing and berating the subordinates with some very colorful language. As they realized a female was present, the sound level became quieter and quieter. The individuals who were drilling the poor presenter suddenly became polite and moved on to the next agenda item, ours. We presented, were questioned politely, and while we weren't giving good news, we were encouraged to keep working on the issue. Several positive suggestions were proposed. As we walked out of the conference room, the next presenter started, and the room reverted to the loud and boisterous talk. I heard a few comments like "who the h—l was that?" The technical leader thanked me for coming, saying "I was right. Having you there kept them from getting mean."

I think about this today as I attend meetings (in businesses, volunteer organizations, or even some local government meetings) filled with men and women. In general, everyone is polite and listens, and there is no overt machoism. However, there are still men who listen to women differently, and it is important to be aware of this, as you want your recommendations to be recognized. I'd like to say it's more common when the man is older and the woman is younger, but that's not always true. So be on the alert for subtle and subliminal actions that can negate your good ideas when you recommend them. (See Chapter 4: "Can You Hear Me Now?")

I included this chapter because everyone's entry into the workplace is different, and while the environment for women in industry has changed, it will continue to morph through time. My first year at IBM, I entered an area that was about as far from an "electric company" as you can get. I fixed problems and made a name for myself as a technical leader. I took risks because I had little to lose at that stage in my career, and I wanted to convince the heavily male-dominated culture that women could do the job. Hopefully, your first assignment will be fun from the day you begin, but if it isn't, don't despair. Give the job a chance and follow the advice in subsequent chapters to get the most out of each experience. I did it, and so can you.

2

STARTING OFF ON THE RIGHT FOOT

In the beginner's mind, there are many possibilities,
but in the expert's there are few.
—*Shunryu Suzuki*

The first chapter described specific issues I dealt with in my first days and months at work. This chapter summarizes what I learned into some general principles for you to consider from day one that will be important to your career success.

Renee's Rules
for Making the Most of Your Early Years

- Work on depth and breadth.
- The earlier you try, the lower the risk.
- Get a mentor and start networking ASAP.
- Portray a can-do attitude.
- Results matter.
- Communicate your results.
- Stay current—technically and professionally.
- Google yourself.

No matter how you map out your future, there will be changes along the way. The best thing you can do in your early years is get as much experience as possible and enhance your technical depth or business skills. You will build on this learning throughout your career, and the problem-solving principles and disciplines you apply early will be invaluable. Learn what databases exist and how to use them, how to justify projects, and the processes and procedures for funding. Learn about return on investment, as every project should have one.

Don't be in a rush to move into management. I see many new engineers believing they can be a manager within a year or so of joining the business, and clearly you can. But considering you are most likely going to work for twenty to thirty years, being a manager in the same area you were working and having only a limited set of business experiences can put you at a disadvantage in the long run. Take on assignments outside your normal sphere of comfort to get as much experience as possible. Start taking risks in your early years, whether a new assignment or an area in which you have no experience. It is easier to bounce back from bumps earlier in your career, and this will prepare you for more significant decisions later.

Rotational assignments also sound nice, but if you move too fast, you don't get a chance to prove your value. On the other hand, if you don't move, then you are seeing the world from only one perspective. It is important to make the most of your early years. Your career path and how senior management views your contributions are intertwined. Understand this as you decide if it makes sense to stay in an area or take on a new assignment.

When I was a teacher, I would pick a day during the year to make students change their seats. Those in front moved to the back, those at the back moved to the front, and they could not sit next to anyone they had previously sat near. On that day, the whole character of the class changed—how students interacted, who answered questions, and more. I tried the same trick at IBM when I became a middle manager. I sat in a different seat, and it forced everyone to try a different perspective. The meeting actually changed character. People who rarely spoke actually participated more. Change your seat, be it in a meeting or in your career, and you, too, will expand your perspective.

Get a mentor. As a new hire, you might start with some sort of buddy who is also a recent hire and can show you the ropes. But after about six months, you should start looking for someone who can advise you in career decisions. Look for a mentor a few levels higher in the business. If your mentor is too high, his or her advice might actually be less helpful than someone a little closer to you in experience. (See Chapter 10: "Will You Be My Mentor?") Also, look for role models in people whom you consider successful and watch how they operate in and out of meetings.

Get onto projects or areas in which key problems are being worked and take any opportunity you can to present to others, especially to management or to customers.

You don't have to wait to be asked to solve problems; just do it in a team approach so others don't feel like you are stepping on their toes. I cannot emphasize this enough: Results matter. Taking on responsibilities and exceeding expectations will make you known and noticed. People like to associate themselves with people who get the job done. Get the job done.

Always project a can-do attitude and never wear your heart on your sleeve. There was nothing worse in my early years than to see a female cry or get upset at work. She would be labeled "emotional," and men veered away from giving her important assignments. Another negative I saw men zoom right in on was lack of confidence or even worse, fear. Never ever show fear. Breathe, prepare, get advice, and remember that the blowhards are just that. The type of image you portray will affect how people want to work with you. Provide solutions rather than complaints. Your attitude can make not just your job but the jobs of those around you more successful. Businesses need committed, capable employees to succeed, and you know more than anyone else about your work. Have faith in your abilities and stand up for them.

Throughout your career, it is important to stay current and keep your technical and business skills honed, so get into good habits right from the start.

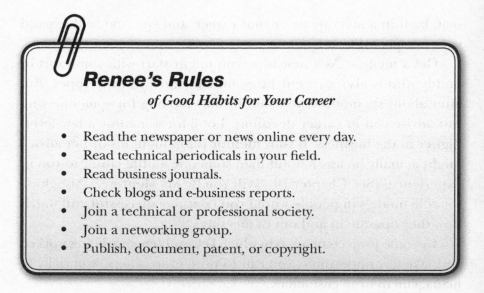

Renee's Rules
of Good Habits for Your Career

- Read the newspaper or news online every day.
- Read technical periodicals in your field.
- Read business journals.
- Check blogs and e-business reports.
- Join a technical or professional society.
- Join a networking group.
- Publish, document, patent, or copyright.

These habits will help keep you current in your profession as well as in life. The connections you make in your early years can be invaluable.

As a beginner, you often see things that others have taken for granted as status quo. You can make a major difference by just trying something no one considered because it had been "done before." Listen more and talk less; you will learn more when you listen. Ask a lot of questions and don't be afraid to ask for help.

Learn as much as you can about your profession and your company. Become an expert, but train others so when the time is right, you can move on to another opportunity without hurting the business.

A new area that employers are now taking advantage of is your Web persona. Google yourself periodically throughout your career. What do you find? Are you there at all? Are the articles and areas in which you are referenced complimentary and accurate? More and more employers and executive headhunters use the Internet as a source of information about employees. Even within the same company, it is common to use one's Internet persona to review candidates for positions. In IBM, as we were reviewing candidates for Distinguished Engineers, a common practice was to include Web data and external impact. Start early and establish yourself as digitally distinctive through external articles, book reviews on Amazon.com, getting engaged in blogs, whatever works. I believe this will be an even more important tool in the future.

Try It Now

Are You Digitally Distinctive?

- Google yourself.

    1. Are you there?
    2. Do you like what you see?

- Check your company's intranet.

    1. Are you there?
    2. Do you like what you see?

- If you find very little or you don't like the tenor of the items, there are many ways to enhance your Internet persona:

    1. Write a book review for Amazon.com or other online press.
    2. Join or start a blog.
    3. Join Linkedin, Facebook or other connections sites.
    4. Create a Web site.
    5. Post accomplishments, meetings where you are the contact person, and other information people will value on your company's intranet.

As you progress in your career, your growth will depend on more than your immediate management chain, but in your early years, your direct supervisor can make a major difference in your future. Many companies have fast-track programs where highfliers are identified early in their careers. This early identification can speed up your career development by having your name known by senior management, making sure you are considered for career growth opportunities, and putting you into situations that will enable you to get more experiences early. Your immediate manager is generally the individual who will recommend you for this program. If you don't know if your company has something like this, ask. If they do have it, ask your manager what it takes to get on it. Establish connections, and always remember to make your manager look good. By this I mean if you act in the way that your manager's measurements are improved, it is for the good of the entire business, not just yourself. As a result, you will have an even greater impact on the business and will be recognized for it.

As a new employee, you may feel that because you are at the bottom of the totem pole, everyone delegates the work downward, and it ends on your shoulders. A common female trap, especially one who has been somewhat of a "control freak," is to accept every assignment and work herself into a frenzy. I mentored a new hire who was such a perfectionist that she not only took on her own tasks, she solved them for others, and was unwilling to hand anything she had perfected over to others for fear they might "mess it up." As a result, she was clearly burning out. It took some time to get her to realize that making the bar so high that no one could do it to her satisfaction was not only an excuse to keep control, but a behavior that demonstrated lack of leadership potential.

Renee's Rules
for Control Freaks

- Being frantic is not being efficient.
- *Good enough* is what your boss or customer needs, not your personal vision of perfection.
- It takes courage to delegate or hand a project over to someone else. Be brave and congratulate yourself for doing so.

Even if you are not a control freak, learning to prioritize and to say no properly will help you find balance. If you find yourself working twelve-plus-hour days and weekends regularly, you will burn out before you have a chance to succeed. Sometimes it is okay to say no. You need to discuss priorities and workload with your manager if you are overloaded, lay out the key projects, your estimate of time involved, and come with a solution you would recommend if you were your manager. The point is to focus on business requirements and priorities in a professional manner rather than complain. If your manager hits you with a request and you know it is not something you can realistically take on, a good answer is "let me think about it and get back to you." This gives you a chance to formulate your issues and say no in a way that shows you are not copping out but doing what makes the most sense.

Try It Now

Saying No

When your boss comes to you with another assignment and you believe you will fail if you add it to your plate, you need to say no. However, there are ways to say this, gain understanding, and demonstrate leadership.

If it is not an earth-shattering event that needs immediate action—like losing a customer or having a technical or business crisis—the best answer is to say, "Let me look into it and get back to you by [give a time frame]. I don't want to commit to something without understanding if I can deliver on it."

Then look at the project—if you can do it and balance other deliverables, say yes. If not, look over the projects you have.

- Can any be delayed?
- Can any be delegated?
- Can any be eliminated?

At the same time, weigh this project against the others you have. Is it something with high visibility or something you'd be excited to work on? If yes, focus on the items above. If not, suggest a different solution to your manager.

- Suggest someone else qualified to do it.
- Suggest an alternative time frame so it can be done when you finish something else.

By suggesting the solution and demonstrating your ability to think like a leader, you will better balance your workload without being negative and keep yourself from overload. Moreover, you are working to help both you and the business succeed.

Robert Louis Stevenson advised that "to get where you want to go, you have to begin where you are." The earlier you learn, the more ingrained good habits become. If you practice the advice in this chapter as you begin your career (although it's never too late to start), you are getting off on the right foot.

3

GREAT MINDS DO NOT
THINK ALIKE

Women discuss, men solve.
—One of my early managers

Having been one of the first female engineers, engineering managers, middle managers, and distinguished engineers in my division, I have spent a lot of time observing both men and women at work. Early on I realized that regardless of industry, company, or technology, there were gender-specific differences in behavior that I needed to be aware of in order to succeed in my mostly male environment. Knowing how to exploit these differences can make you a better employee and leader. A woman does not have to act like a man to succeed, but understanding what male and female behaviors are more effective in a given situation will allow you to use these differences to your advantage. In addition, for a male leader, understanding the subtle differences in how the sexes think, react, and solve problems can make his team that much more effective.

There are countless books and articles about the physiological differences between the left and right brain, and how women and men favor one versus the other. I don't claim to be an expert in this, nor do I want to debate "nurture versus nature," but I do think that understanding these differences is important. Most studies indicate that women can connect the two hemispheres of the brain more effectively (and are therefore more intuitive and able to multitask), while men are better at abstract problems. Other experts have concluded that boys and girls are trained in society differently. As a young girl, I remember my mother and teachers often telling me to "play nice" when I had a disagreement with my friends. I also heard, "Share," "It's not nice to be bossy," "Don't interrupt," and other comments essentially emphasizing that young girls should work together and not order each other around. As I got older, aggressive or demanding behavior was deemed "not ladylike." Young men, on the other hand, grow up in a much more competitive environment. They are told, "Don't be a sissy," "Aren't you a big, strong boy?", "Boys don't cry," and similar comments. Boys' toys are bats, balls, and trucks while girls are given dolls, paints, and dress-up clothes.

Perhaps this is changing, but as I observe young children at play, I doubt it. I recently attended a birthday party for a four-year-old held at an indoor baseball arena. The little boys went right into the games, throwing and kicking the balls, while the girls generally held the balls and stayed on the sidelines. When the children were given bats to swing at a candy piñata, the boys attacked the target with all their strength. The girls (every one of them) gave the piñata a light tap with the bat and then dropped it quickly. Frankly, with all the awareness today of gender behaviors as children, I would have hoped to have seen at least one or two girls smack that piñata, but alas none did. Even my own granddaughter, then nineteen months old, was much more interested in the drawings on the balls than with throwing them. More recently, at two, she was playing a game of "giant step" with a friend. After she won twice, I suggested we try a game of "red light, green light." My granddaughter responded, "First, we have to play one more game of giant steps so Lacey has a chance to win." Tell me little girls aren't already programmed differently.

You can say this is hogwash, and before I started working in a largely male environment, I felt that way as well. Now I am much more sensitized to the differences and have observed them almost everywhere. A few years ago, as a Women in Technology representative from IBM to a large university, I was asked to participate in a summer workshop for high school girls and give the keynote address. During the week, the girls were given a challenging problem, to build a boat out of cardboard and duct tape. Teams competed to build and then row their entry around a swimming pool. The winning team was the one whose boat managed the longest time above water without sinking as the cardboard got soggy. I observed one particular high school girl putting herself completely into the project, directing the team, recommending very creative solutions, and clearly demonstrating a high leadership potential. I was really impressed. Her team won the competition. The final night, family and friends were invited to the celebration. After my keynote address, I went over to this individual to comment upon her excellent performance. This time, however, the young lady's boyfriend was at the dinner table. It was as though an alien personality had occupied her body. Suddenly she became cutesy and appeared much less knowledgeable about buoyancy, water absorption, and the other factors she was assessing as she designed her boat.

My final example comes from Donald Trump. In the first season of *The Apprentice*, I watched several episodes of the show. In the first challenges, the teams consisted of all-male and all-female teams. In each episode, the women came out on top. As a result, after a few weeks, the teams were rearranged to be coed. After that, the women started being the ones "fired." Did the women behave differently when working in teams with men? Did they not get the subliminal differences and as such perform more poorly? I cannot ignore this possibility. Please understand, I am not saying you need to think about gender differences all the time, but I do believe that your awareness of the differences can help you find the best way to lead and deal with people depending on the situation.

Another area that concerns me is that some men still have a tendency to consider their partner's working as the icing on the cake or more of a hobby than a requirement, despite the huge number of working women today. Educators and guidance counselors may also unconsciously apply dual standards. As a member of the Society of Women Engineers, we started a program to bring hands-on science education techniques to middle school teachers. This program showed women as science role models to the teachers and also made them more comfortable with science as experimentation. In IBM and other large companies, programs such as EXCITE Camps, which bring middle school girls into industry for a week of science camp, are also excellent ways to encourage more girls to pursue science as a career. When we stop needing activities of this type, then I will know we have succeeded in changing the cultural inhibitors.

Whether the source is societal or genetic, awareness of these behavioral differences will help maximize your effectiveness. Many books have been written about these differences. In the video, *The Power-Dead Even Rule*, Pat Heim asserts that men are hierarchical while women look for equals. A woman automatically considers what seems fair, while that may not occur to a man at all. (I am not implying men are selfish; they just don't naturally think this way.) Women talk it over and use the process of talking to work out problems. Girls are encouraged to be modest, so they are "even" with their peers, while boys are encouraged to lead and negotiate their rank by challenging others and resisting threats to their authority. As a result, they hesitate to ask for help. One example of this difference frequently happened to me and my husband when we would travel. If we found ourselves lost despite all our maps and written directions, I would suggest stopping at a gas station or asking a pedestrian for directions, something my husband was loath to do. We had some very heated discussions over this until I realized this was a normal gender difference. We now have a GPS. Problem solved!

In *Men Are from Mars, Women Are from Venus*, John Gray describes how a woman might suggest to her partner that they "go shopping" as a process and an opportunity to spend time together, while her partner sees "going shopping" as going to a store, buying an item, and leaving. This leads to conflict and disappointment. The same behaviors can cause issues at work. One of my bosses used to say, "Women like to ask questions; men like to give answers." Women are excellent problem solvers, but they often arrive at an answer from a different direction. Men, on the other hand, come to a decision quickly and then often have no patience with discussion on what they consider a solved problem.

For example, a woman often sees a meeting as a place to bring her concerns and discuss options to come to the best answer. A man, on the other hand, will often do his lobbying and decision-making before the meeting and come in ready to move forward with what he has already gotten agreement to do, not recognizing this can lead women to be very disappointed in the outcome of a meeting. I have learned to always check out in advance the agendas of any upper-level meetings. I do some discussions with participants ahead of time to be sure a hidden agenda or prior agreement will not take me by surprise. (More on this in Chapter 4: "Can You Hear Me Now?")

Another source of frustration on the job occurs because men and women may use the same words, but mean them differently. The first time in my career my manager asked me to join a task force "team," I went expecting to hear a discussion of the problem and to be asked about ways we could correct it. Instead, at the meeting the "team leader" put up a mini organization chart describing who would perform what roles in order to resolve the issues. I was somewhat surprised to see my name next to a position that was not really how I felt I could best contribute to the solution and wasn't sure what my "role" really was.

Many books have been written about these subtle differences in word meanings. So I will just summarize some examples that clearly affected me.

Renee's Rules
for Words and Expressions to Use Carefully to Avoid Misunderstandings

- Team
- Power
- Success
- Thank you
- What do you think?
- Can you help?

Let's discuss some of the confusion each of these can cause, starting with *team*. A man naturally thinks in terms of sports, so to him a team is a number of people playing their positions. When he attends a task force team kickoff, he expects to be given his position or assignment. A woman naturally thinks of a team as a group of people working together regardless of position. She expects the team to figure out the roles once they understand the problem.

The word *power* has subtly different meanings depending on gender. A man thinks of power as his ability to drive others to do what he wants, often based on his position in the organization. A woman thinks of power as the ability to convince others to do what she wants, regardless of her level. Very similar and at the same time, oh so different.

Success is another word that can bring two different meanings to men and women. A male defines it as winning, beating the competition, or achieving a specific position or salary. Women define success more intrinsically, wanting to show their value and be recognized for it. A subtle demonstration of this occurred for me when two people I knew well were promoted to a major technical position. The male came to thank me for my support, starting with the words, "I made senior engineer." The female came later in the same day and stated, "I was appointed to senior engineer." The difference is subtle, but the male clearly claimed more credit for the same promotion than the female did.

Saying *thank you* may seem like a very basic comment that can't cause any gender differences, right? Wrong! Women like to be thanked often, with small comments that don't single them out in a crowd. Men will generally look at frequent thanking as reducing the impact of your appreciation. Moreover, they like to be thanked in public.

Another difference that can cause dissatisfaction occurs when you ask a woman or man, *What do you think?* A woman often interprets the question as the opening of a conversation. A man will respond with what he considers the answer, not surprising based on how the sexes solve problems differently. If a woman asks "What do you think?" as a conversation opener and gets a terse solution from a male, she may feel very frustrated. The male, on the other hand, feels he did exactly what was asked of him and can't understand why she's upset.

I experienced this recently when I accompanied a friend and her husband as they shopped for appliances. She was clearly leaning toward a specific brand, but her husband didn't realize it. She asked him, "What do you think?" fully expecting him to start a conversation with her about the brands. However, he answered, "Let's get the GE." My friend did not prefer that brand but was now put into the position of having to defend her choice or just let it go. They bought the GE.

My final example is, *Can you help?* When a man hears those words, he waits to hear what help you had in mind and will assist with what he can do. When a woman hears those words, she wants to understand the problem and will often do more than asked.

These distinctions may seem small, but they can lead to friction in the workplace. Your male boss may ask you to be on a team, expecting you to fulfill a specific role, while you think of the assignment as more amorphous, developing shape as the project needs become more defined. Discussing up front exactly what it means to be on the team is essential to making sure you meet his expectations. And if you are a female boss asking a male to join a team, he may be looking for you to define his position and be confused when you are ambiguous.

Similarly, if a female comes to a meeting to discuss a problem and expects to work out the solution there, the men may become impatient or feel she is wasting their valuable time, while she walks out feeling she was ignored.

There are better approaches to avoid these pitfalls. If a female wants to discuss an issue but doesn't want it solved for her, a much better tactic than asking, "What do you think?" is to instead ask, "Can I use you for a sounding board? I have several approaches I am thinking about to solve this problem and need someone to talk them out with." If, on the other hand, a male wants a quick yes or no, a better way to pose the question is, "Do you agree?"

In the case of my appliance shopping friend, she should have said, "I think I like the XXX better than the other brands because of YYY. Am I missing anything that would make me choose something else?"

Men should also be aware that women often ask, "What do you think?" when they have completed something successfully, expecting to receive a short compliment like, "Good job." If a man proceeds to find fault, however small, when the woman expected to hear positive feedback, she may walk away deflated rather than excited over her accomplishment.

My personal belief is that the differences between how men and women think are extremely advantageous to an organization and are a fundamental reason why including women in leadership positions enhances the overall organization. They solve problems differently and can bring a different perspective, which makes everyone's approach stronger. This different perspective can make the end solution even more robust and successful, especially if the product is going to be used by both men and women. Use the differences to your organization's advantage!

Let's get back to problem solving. Studies show that men and women do solve problems differently. A man's desire for a quick decision, be it on a shopping trip or at work, often causes conflict when a female feels she needs to complete the "process." Men have little patience for further discussion when they feel the issue has been solved. They consider these lengthy discourses a waste of their valuable time. It is important to recognize the warning signs that this is happening and to *stop talking*. If you've lost your audience, you will be losing rather than gaining ground in trying to discuss the issue further.

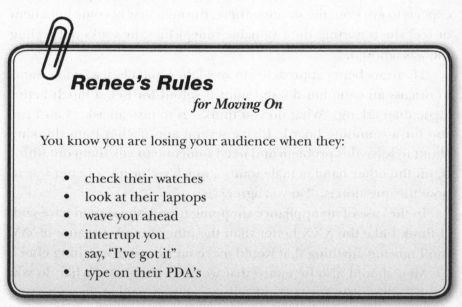

Renee's Rules
for Moving On

You know you are losing your audience when they:

- check their watches
- look at their laptops
- wave you ahead
- interrupt you
- say, "I've got it"
- type on their PDA's

Another mistake women commonly make is in assuming others know what they want. Women expect that if they do a good job, it will be recognized, and they will be appropriately rewarded. They hate to toot their own horns. Men don't assume, and they make sure to tell others what they want. Very often I will mentor a female engineer and ask about her projects. She will describe the contributions of others on the team and the overall outcome without specifically identifying her contribution. A male engineer with the same years with IBM will generally describe his projects in terms of what he specifically did. This "I" versus "we" is great to enable a team, but can lead to women receiving less recognition than they deserve. My husband regularly reminds his boss he is underpaid whenever he lands a new contract or pulls off a business coup. He does it in a teasing manner, but keeps the issue in his boss's mind. I have never been so comfortable in that role but have tried to emulate it in the right situations, and it has worked. (See Chapter 8: Dare I Ask? Negotiating for Yourself.)

Try It Now

Tooting Your Horn

- Make a list of what you work on for an entire week. Just jot down the items with no analysis.
- At the end of the week, review what you worked on.

1. Which had significant impact or potential for your career or the business?
2. Who knows what you did?
3. Who understands the significance?

If no one knows what you did and its importance, you need to find ways to share it. Who would benefit from knowing your results? Send them an update or schedule a short meeting to share the results.

I have known men in many industries and businesses who held women back because they believed women were wives and mothers first. Again there are more enlightened managers today, but don't just assume you are working for one. In my early years, I had one manager who never told me about job offers because he was positive that I would not want to relocate (my husband had a job in the area, and my children were in elementary school). This same manager didn't hesitate to inform a man with a working wife and children in school about those opportunities. When I found out about this, I made sure I had a conversation with the manager that I wanted to be aware of any opportunities, local or otherwise, and make my own decisions. And I have done so with every new individual I worked for since then. But the best way to do this is by working with your manager or boss on a development plan that is updated annually. If your firm does this as a personnel practice, great—make the most of it. If not, schedule appropriate time with your manager or boss to discuss your future.

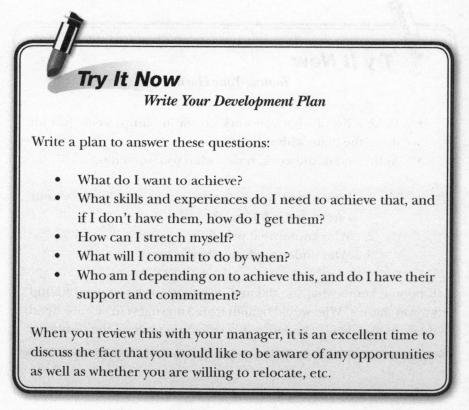

Try It Now
Write Your Development Plan

Write a plan to answer these questions:

- What do I want to achieve?
- What skills and experiences do I need to achieve that, and if I don't have them, how do I get them?
- How can I stretch myself?
- What will I commit to do by when?
- Who am I depending on to achieve this, and do I have their support and commitment?

When you review this with your manager, it is an excellent time to discuss the fact that you would like to be aware of any opportunities as well as whether you are willing to relocate, etc.

A friend had an even more blatant experience in another company. She applied for an assignment and was told she wasn't chosen because she had children! I suggested she respond, "Then I assume that a man with children would also be excluded?" She decided she did not want to work for this individual, and made sure that her manager and HR were aware of these comments so appropriate action could be taken.

Recently, a young female I was coaching complained to me about a slightly different situation, where her supervisor decided for her without asking. She was an expert in a particular groundbreaking technical area and was doing a great deal of work in it. When a task force was formed to accelerate the learning in this area, she was not asked to lead either the task force or any of the subteams. She asked her manager about it, and he indicated that she was "so busy" with her regular work that he did not think she could take on any more. When she asked him if he felt she wasn't qualified to lead this, he said, "No, that's definitely not the case." I advised her to have a frank discussion with him that he should have consulted her before declining this opportunity for her. Perhaps she would have been willing to take this on. Perhaps she could have off-loaded some of the more mundane tasks. Perhaps she was willing to give extra hours. Or perhaps she would have come to the very same conclusion her manager did. Regardless, he took the power to decide away from her and, as such, a potential opportunity at future recognition and significant technical enhancement. After we spoke, she went back to her manager and proposed a realignment of responsibilities so she could co-chair one of the teams. He considered her proposal, agreed with it, and gave her the opportunity she desired. Equally important, her manager understood that in the future, he needed to involve her in any such decisions.

Does a woman have to change to a man's character to succeed? Yes and no.

It is not necessary to obsess about the differences between men and women, but it is important for a woman to consider how the men she is working with think. If you know that your boss is looking for quick answers at a meeting, spend your time prior to the meeting getting to your recommendation, even if you need to use someone else as your sounding board. If you are feeling guilty about assigning work to your male team and instead take more on yourself, output will suffer. On the other hand, by being more approachable and sensitive to inhibitors to good work, a woman can help her team stay on the right path and overcome problems before they become large. Work on the female strengths while understanding the male expectations, and you will have the best of both worlds. One of my friends calls it "combining soft and hard."

Finally, when you are one of the few women in a largely male area, it is important to remember that you are a role model. Men will watch if you can succeed, and women will try to emulate your success. It takes a long time to overcome their biases, even if they recognize them. When a friend's daughter started working in her first internship, she was surprised to find out that she was being given easier projects than her male counterparts when, in fact, her GPA was better than theirs. When she confronted her manager, he actually admitted that he was judging her by a prior summer intern, also blond and cute, who spent more time flirting than getting the job done. As such, he gave this cute blond female fewer meaningful assignments. Without consciously thinking about it, her supervisor transferred his bad experience to biasing his opinion about the woman's capability. After she confronted him, he corrected this, but this bias lasted for many months. Be a positive role model, work to bust any unfair prejudices others may not even realize they have, and you will help those who follow.

P.S. I finished writing this chapter a few days before Christmas, and at one of the meetings I attended earlier that day, I observed another behavioral difference. In the meeting were eight men and two women. Both women had completed their shopping; as for the men, the eight had not yet started. Tell me men and women don't think differently!

4

CAN YOU HEAR ME NOW?

Half the world is composed of people who have something
to say and can't, and the other half who have nothing to say
and keep on saying it

—*Robert Frost*

A very important trait for making your point in a business or technical world is how you speak, as that affects how your audience listens to you. You will know they aren't listening if you find yourself making a suggestion in a meeting, no one picks up on it, then later someone else suggests the exact same thing, and everyone thinks it's a great idea! This is one of those subtle behaviors that I have seen, and many people don't even realize it is happening. This seems to happen more often to women, especially if they do not come to the point right away. What's worse, I have even observed a woman going through exactly what I just described above, being ignored in a meeting. Then shortly after her comment, a male suggested the same thing, and everyone agreed with the proposal. This woman told me after the meeting that she felt really great because she got the end result she wanted. Yes, *she* felt good but *he* got the recognition for the solution!

In business and technical meetings, how you say what you are trying to convey can affect the degree with which others agree with you. Women naturally voice their doubts more often than men. (It comes from "talking it out.") Busy senior managers and executives must make decisions quickly, often from listening for just a few minutes, so get to the point with strong convictions. Remember, you know your topic better than anyone else, so act like it. Emanate confidence.

If you are one of those people who gets nervous before a major presentation or meeting where you have to present, this story might help you. In my early years when I would present at an all-hands meeting in a large auditorium, I would actually feel my heartbeat going faster, and even with a few deep breaths, it took me a while to get into my presentations so that I felt comfortable. I shared this concern with a very eloquent rabbi who always gave the most confident and moving sermons. I asked him how he kept from getting nervous when he started. He looked at me somewhat astonished and said, "Renee, I am always nervous before a sermon, and I am so glad that I am. It reminds me that I care." Ever since then, when I get those flutters, I remind myself that this means I care about what I am going to say, and it helps me relax (a bit).

Besides a confident, factual, no-nonsense delivery, there are other ways to help make sure your ideas are heard. If it is a meeting where presentations are being shown, make sure to put your idea down in writing in a clear statement but not one that explains everything (then they have to listen to you for further clarification). For example, suppose there is considerable discussion going on for your business problem, be it technical, customer-related, personnel-related, or whatever. Put a chart together and stand up. (Yes, people do listen better if you stand up in front of the room when you present.) The chart should state the problem and a cursory statement about your solution. Then when you have their attention you say, "Let me explain more clearly." Now everyone is listening, and if the idea is good, they know it came from you.

Renee's Rules
for Speaking

- Talk to the audience, not your presentation.
- Never "read" your presentation.
- Stand up.
- Modulate your voice.
- Make eye contact or look across heads.
- Watch body language.
- Don't put your hands in your pockets.

Your voice can affect the way people listen to you. There may be times that you want to raise it to the levels of others, but once you have their attention, you can often be more effective by lowering your voice so people need to really pay attention to listen. Cultural norms and behaviors can affect how individuals speak. For example, Asian American women tend to speak softly and very respectfully. Here, modulating your voice can be even more effective as when you speak out of your normal character people will notice the difference. You don't want to sound confrontational, but you do want to convey your point. In a larger group, avoid specific eye contact but rather look across the heads. Focusing in on one person may derail your thoughts if that person yawns, makes a face, or turns to speak to a neighbor. And never ever speak with your head down.

Reading your slides insults your listeners since they can read faster than you can speak. As such, they will often read ahead when you put a chart or presentation in front of them. Busy senior managers and executives want to hear from you, not listen to you read.

When you are presenting, use data whenever possible to demonstrate your point. Data is gender neutral, and everyone will react positively. Data is much more effective than opinion.

Renee's Rules
for Controlling Your Presentation

- Prevent them (and you) from reading ahead by only putting reminders or key words on your slides.
- Tell them up front what you are going to tell them.
- Tell them, incorporating stories along the way,
- Tell them at the end what you told them.

By putting the bare minimum you need to stay on point on your slides, you prevent getting caught reading, and you also prevent others from reading ahead. By telling a story, you keep them involved. And by summarizing in the beginning and again at the end, you make sure they leave with the message you want them to remember. It's okay to have key phases on the presentation, but *not to* have the full explanation there. I like to summarize data and put the details in the backup. Doing it this way allows you to control the pace of the discussion. This is even more important today, as presentations are often online and many meetings are remote. People read ahead and may tune you out before you get to the punch line. The less they can do this because you use the slides as an outline, not the whole story, the more control you will have in the delivery.

By the way, some people disagree with my approach because they claim that a presentation should be able to make its point without having the author present. The argument is that it might get included by someone else in another presentation and should therefore be self-explanatory. I still disagree. If someone else is incorporating your work into theirs, how can you be sure they are drawing the same conclusions, and why are they presenting your work anyway?

Learning to "net it" and convince people in just a few words is critical in today's fast-paced business. Executives and clients are busy people, and they do not have time for detailed explanations. If a presentation is too complex and too long, the listener has to search for your message. Lou Gerstner, former IBM CEO, insisted that anyone coming to present to him keep it to only two pages! One of my mentors at IBM told me often, "If you can't net it, you don't know it."

Try It Now

Say It in a Few Words

- Review the last presentation you gave.

- Now in one sentence, what was the message you wanted the listener to hear?

- Did you put that message up front and again at the end?

- Did everything you show support that message?

- Cut your presentation to two slides.

Even if you end up giving a longer presentation, doing this exercise keeps your focus on the main point. Whenever I am giving a presentation, I start with two slides and expand from there.

Knowing when to stop talking is another important piece of advice. When you have made your points and everyone is agreeing, that's when you should stop talking. I have seen many people, especially women, keep on talking when they have won over their audience and, in so doing, bring up a point that then forces them back into having to justify their position. Stop talking when you've won!

Let's go back to being heard. Make sure you look at the audience, especially if you have an accent, speak softly, or have trouble keeping everyone's attention. I recently watched a young female engineer try to walk up to the front of the conference room, but because someone had his legs stretched out, she was forced to present in an uncomfortable location. She could not look at both the senior executive to whom she was presenting and the screen where her presentation was being projected at the same time. From this unnatural position, she frequently turned her back to the screen or her audience, interrupting her train of thought. Since she also had a thick accent, much of what she said was missed. This may seem like a small thing, but you must communicate effectively no matter what the discipline or business. If you start with a disadvantage like a strong accent, you need to make sure everything else works in your favor.

If all else fails and you still find your ideas are being ignored, get an advocate before the meeting. In fact, you are probably not preparing for meetings properly, so here are some rules to help you.

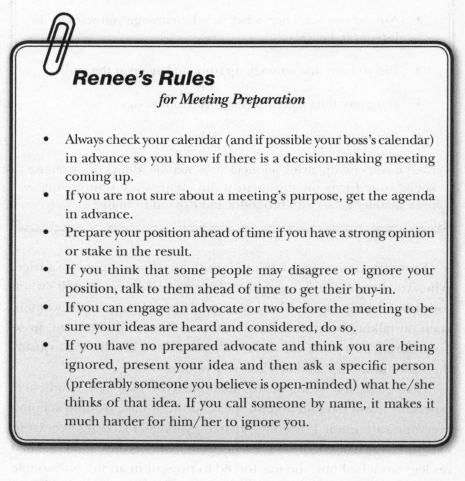

Renee's Rules
for Meeting Preparation

- Always check your calendar (and if possible your boss's calendar) in advance so you know if there is a decision-making meeting coming up.
- If you are not sure about a meeting's purpose, get the agenda in advance.
- Prepare your position ahead of time if you have a strong opinion or stake in the result.
- If you think that some people may disagree or ignore your position, talk to them ahead of time to get their buy-in.
- If you can engage an advocate or two before the meeting to be sure your ideas are heard and considered, do so.
- If you have no prepared advocate and think you are being ignored, present your idea and then ask a specific person (preferably someone you believe is open-minded) what he/she thinks of that idea. If you call someone by name, it makes it much harder for him/her to ignore you.

This may sound like a lot of planning and manipulation, and I certainly wouldn't expect you to do this for every meeting. But I have found men do this much more often than you think. Two voices are much harder to ignore than one.

The last item above, singling out a specific person, is something I learned in a self-defense class. If someone is mugged or attacked, rather than yelling "somebody help me," pick out a specific person in the crowd. Calling, "Will you in the blue shirt help me?" makes it harder for the person in the blue shirt to ignore you. A similar principle works here.

A common behavior in today's wireless world is to be presenting at a meeting while the audience is busy looking at its laptops. Again, this is done to both men and women, but I find for some reason women tend to tolerate it more. Don't. Assess the audience. If no one is listening, there's no point in talking! I have found that when I stand up and look like I'm ready to present but don't actually start, someone usually asks what I am waiting for. I respond very pleasantly, "I am waiting for you to finish your e-mail so I can begin." It's important to take the stage, meaning that you get control and make sure people are listening to you before you start. On the other hand, if a senior manager waves you to go ahead and he/she is looking at a laptop or other papers, start talking. Hopefully the story you tell will get him or her to look up. If you refer to people by name as you describe something, they will often look up. Once you have their interest, it is easier to keep it.

When you are at a meeting, respect other speakers by minimizing the chatter. If you are making comments often, then when you really want to make your point, you will have a greater chance of being ignored. Right or wrong, most men do not tolerate chatter from women or other men.

Say what you mean. Being subtle leads to being misunderstood.

Finally, don't start your comments with "I think" or "in my opinion." If you are saying it, it is your opinion, and the point comes across much stronger if you just say it. The more confidence you exude, the more the audience will believe you.

As you move up in your career, you will find that you need to make more critical presentations, speak to larger groups, get to the point quicker, and do more lobbying for support outside meetings. This skill is every bit as important as your technical or business ability, so spend the time to perfect it.

5

SOME LEADERS
ARE BORN WOMEN

*By working faithfully eight hours a day, you may eventually
get to be a boss and work twelve hours a day.*

—*Robert Frost*

There is a shift in how many businesses are being run today. Collaboration and cooperation are replacing command and control, exactly the style of leadership women do naturally. Leadership requirements have not changed but leadership styles have.

Male or female, to lead you must be competent and qualified. You must be able to articulate a vision yet look for consensus. Most importantly, after you hear it all, you must be willing to make the decisions and bear the responsibility for your choice. Regardless of gender, leaders need to be confident, rational, thick-skinned, and empowering of others. Good leaders know how to match their style to the needs of their employees, customers, or coworkers, especially in today's global multicultural society. They understand what makes their employees passionate. They promote cooperation between employees and between teams. One of my senior managers told me good leaders enforce reality and offer hope. True leaders believe in their people, so their people believe in them. A true leader awakens the possibilities in others.

While leaders share many "must dos," there are many different styles of leaders in the workplace, and gender differences can create subtle distinctions. Studies indicate that as leaders, men tend to be transactional:

"Do this because I said so" or "because it's needed." When they disagree with a transactional leader, some employees respond with a loop-four behavior. That is, they do what they are told but secretly hope it fails.

Women tend to be more transformational, seeking employee buy-in. Studies show that employees working for a transformational leader, male or female, tend to be more effective in the long term because they believe in what they are doing and do their best to achieve it. However, when faced with a particularly challenging assignment where employees are under-prepared for their new roles, transactional leadership can be more effective. Again, there is no "right" leadership style. Good leaders know which to use when. Male or female, leaders can augment their effectiveness if they know how to maximize use of the right style.

Men and women can differ in their definition of leader, just as they differ in their concept of team. Remember, women excel at consensus and working to get everyone on the same page while men consider leadership as a more hierarchical concept, with a span of control and number of employees measuring the leader's importance. They will talk about winning, while the women leaders will talk about success. As a manager, if you can adjust your style to encourage both behaviors, you will excel.

In many technical companies, one can choose to pursue a technical or a managerial career path. Both, however, involve leadership. In today's highly interactive and global economy, business and technical success cannot happen without leadership skills. So even if you choose (or chose) a nonmanagerial role, many of the elements of leadership and management discussed in this chapter apply to you. Managers must learn to empower and trust their technical leaders, and technical leaders must be held accountable for all aspects of the business. These two very important and very different groups have a history of not always working together. It is imperative for you to foster a common strategy whichever side you are on and be an active proponent of the company's policies. As you grow in your career responsibility, your depth of leadership should also grow.

I wavered back and forth during my career, going into and out of management more than once. I also moved to a third-level management assignment but dropped to a second because it was something that I saw as a challenge. (In IBM, a manager with direct employee reports is called a first level or line, a manager of managers is called a second level, a manager of second level managers is a third level, etc.) Take the assignment that sounds like a challenge and the "level" will work itself out. The path of your career will have a lot of meanderings along the way, and that's perfectly fine if the side trips are doing something that helps hone your skills, makes a difference for the business, or fits the work/life-balancing situation you happen to be in at that time.

After a few years in IBM, my third-level manager offered me a management position. I had led several task forces by that time, and he was impressed with my leadership abilities in those assignments, but it was still a man's world. I was the second woman technical manager at the particular IBM facility and the first in the manufacturing and equipment engineering discipline. My first department was 100 percent male. My third line told me that he was willing to "take a chance on me." Then he added, "You'd better be good because as the first woman, you know that everyone will be watching you." Phew—that was a heavy weight to put on my first assignment, but I guess I did a good job as within a few years more women managers started appearing in the engineering disciplines. Today, the population of women in technical management in IBM closely matches the percentage of women in technical positions. I like to think I had some small impact on that.

Going into management early in my career had some definite plusses, but there are also some solid reasons to wait. In my situation, I was already older with considerable teaching experience, and I felt I had what it took to do the job. However, going into management early can put you at a disadvantage, not technically but in understanding people and the way your business runs. I generally feel an individual needs a minimum of two technical/business assignments before becoming a manager, and likewise it is good practice to manage several departments before becoming a second-line manager. I see many new hires anxious to enter management. The reality is that in your early years, more than any other, you have the opportunity to move around with minimal impact on your long-term career, and you will enhance your skills and business understanding by doing so. If you are going to work for thirty-plus years, does it really matter if you enter management at year three or five or seven? On the other hand, if an exciting opportunity comes along and you feel you are ready, why wait?

As I started my first managerial assignment, I spent some time considering how I wanted to manage. I reached the conclusion early on that I really didn't want to manage, but I wanted to lead and facilitate (probably a throwback to my power dead-even tendencies). As an ex-teacher, I felt if I gave good people the education, tools, desire, and opportunity, they'd succeed. I tried to provide that. This was not the norm in the all-male community, but the men working for me responded extremely well to this (as did women engineers as they started to arrive). Perhaps it's the nurturing skills women are taught in our society or the fact that I'd been a parent and a teacher by the time I became a manager, but I have always felt my job was to help my employees grow. At various times I was teasingly called "Mom" by my employees, but I took it as a compliment. I remember one employee saying he'd walk through fire for me and would have set his previous manager on fire!

Women have an inherent ability to listen, a concern for relationships and teamwork, and a willingness to compromise for the good of the whole that is not an instinctive behavior for a macho male. My older daughter recently became a manager in another technical company, and I had to smile when she told me her employees had called her "Mom." History is repeating itself.

Why did I go into management? I loved the technical leadership and being in the forefront of technical learning. However, I felt that I could have a greater impact as a manager since I would see a much-broader perspective. What was hard in those early years as a manager was deciding when to take charge and when to step back. Managing people means letting them grow, which means you have to be willing to "give up the reins." From a practical perspective, if you don't do this, you will never get your work done, will end up with one-hundred-hour workweeks, and will burn yourself out. (More on delegating later.) It is a "fine dance" between over-managing and making sure your employees are getting the job done. And it will change depending on the employee and the particular assignment that employee is given. It is not at all unusual to find an employee can be completely capable and drive one activity with essentially no assistance from management, while in another situation this same employee needs significant guidance.

Being the only woman manager during my early years did have one clear advantage. Whenever there was an off-site managers' meeting, the ladies' room was never crowded. Seriously, as a new woman manager, I worked hard on leadership and people management skills and almost never thought about being a "woman" manager.

In my early days as a manager, I received a considerable amount of training in IBM. Much of it involved IBM practices and beliefs; but this was well-balanced with people management skills, psychology, problem solving, team building, and the importance of understanding what motivates people. This is outside the scope of a book about working in a man's world, but I do want to highlight some of the classes in which I got advice or skills that lasted throughout my career. I found situational leadership an excellent class that gave me tools to lead people by understanding their willingness (attitude) and readiness (skills) to take on an assignment and adjusting my style accordingly. Other classes in management styles, coaching, effective listening, and business management were invaluable. Not every company provides this type of assistance, but I recommend you at least search out some management training books if you have no method to get formal training. Also, model yourself after managers whom you found to be effective for you. Think about the techniques they used when you were frustrated, excited, concerned about risk taking, happy, or upset, and try to emulate them.

Another area where women naturally excel is in making their employees feel recognized and rewarded. Throughout the years, my bosses often came to me to organize employee recognition events. It wasn't that they considered it women's work; it was that they realized I was better at it than they were. Recognizing people's skills and pushing for team contribution and recognition contributes to a very positive working climate and will pay back even more in the long run.

As a new manager, there was a lot for me to learn, even though I had been leading teams for some time. One of my first realizations was that not all my employees were driven by the same things that excited me. I remember giving my first promotion. I had been attending management school all week when the promotion approval came through. I was so excited for him that I made a special point to stop at work at the end of the day on the way back from school to give the employee his promotion. I called him into my office, told him what a good job he had been doing and as a result he was being promoted.

I thought it was a big deal; he was getting a healthy increase and an important level change. He looked at the sheet of paper with the particulars, looked at me, and said, "okay." He then proceeded to walk out the door. There was no thank you, no smile, not a glimmer of the excitement I had felt about the promotion. This was clearly an eye-opener for me to try to understand what really mattered to employees and not to put my own values onto them.

The second area where I had to improve my skills as a new manager was in delegating. This is another fine line where I see women and men behaving differently. Since men are more command oriented and see people in roles more distinctly, they are more comfortable giving out assignments. Because women tend to be less worried about boundaries and positions, they are excellent at empowering their employees and usually very approachable. (I often had employees tell me they felt they could confide something to me that they were never able to share with their prior managers, and as such, we were able to overcome their particular inhibitors more quickly.) However, this can backfire when it comes to delegating. Don't be so open and approachable that people tend to dump their problems back on you.

When I attended IBM management school shortly after my first managerial assignment, they ended the class with a very clever presentation on "who has the monkey?" The presenter actually put a stuffed monkey on his shoulder, and we role-played several manager-employee interactions. The person with the monkey was the one who ended up with the problem on their shoulders after the discussion. If you are too empathetic, you may end up doing the work (wearing the monkey) when it is much more appropriate that the employee does so. This doesn't have to be a manager-employee interaction. When you are trying to divide up the work, think about who is wearing the monkey and make sure you aren't the only one doing it.

When I started in management, I spent too much time empathizing with my employees. I felt I was overloading them (even if they never indicated an issue). I did some assignments they could easily have handled. I also fell into the trap of feeling good when I finished them. (It's a more direct and positive feedback when *you* do something well than when it is done by your employees.) Finally, I felt some tasks were too important to risk giving to someone else. So, I found myself staying at work later and later. My employees would pass by my office saying good night, and I'd still be there with a good hour or two more of work to finish, and then even more to take home. I finally realized that if I tried to keep up this pace, I would burn out before a year was up and got some guidance on how to delegate more effectively. Here are some points that helped me.

Renee's Rules
for Successful Delegating

- Divide the work.
- Be specific.
- Inspect, don't expect.

  1. How will you measure progress?
  2. How often will you measure progress?

- Ask who, what, why, when, how, and where.
- Know what support your employees are depending on, from you or others

The first trap I fell into was deciding whom to assign what. When I started giving assignments or holding meetings where I tried to divide up the work, I found that some individuals volunteered for everything (and didn't necessarily get the work done), while others who were very competent waited to be asked. If you have not done this, step back and review the members of your department: their skills, the resources available to them, their workload, and who the "go to" person would be for the various areas of responsibility. After understanding everyone's workload and key responsibilities, as new demands come in, you will quickly determine who is best equipped and sufficiently free to handle the work (not always the same person).

After giving out a few projects, I quickly learned that communication of expectations is critically important. When you delegate, you need to be specific. The more you can describe the expectation—how it will be measured, when it needs to be done, and how you want feedback—the more likely you will get what you want. However, this should not be a top-down, "do this" discussion. Listening to your employees' questions and concerns will help you get their buy-in, make sure you are both on the same page in terms of expectations and how the work will be done, and assure that what you have asked for is realistic. Be sure to ask what help the employee may need, if appropriate, and discuss how you want feedback.

A senior manager advised me early on to "inspect, don't expect." By this he meant never assume that something is being done—establish checkpoints and feedback to assure it is happening. If you agree up front with your employees to do this and make the measurements part of the normal business environment rather than a perception of checking up on them, what you want to be completed will be completed.

As I delegated more and more to employees, giving assignments got easier and easier. It helped to ask the same questions newspaper reporters used, namely, who, what, why, when, how, and where. Specifically decide *who* will do the work, *what* is needed, *why* the person selected is the right one for the job, *when* the work needs to be completed, and *how* you would like to receive interim reports on the progress. If the employee worked remotely or our team spanned multiple locations, I also included *where.* Using these questions assured that my employees understood my expectations, and I better understood their points. Before I knew it, I was walking out the door at the same time as my employees, and my department was getting more accomplished with less rework. (Although I do have to admit, I did take home some personnel work from time to time.)

Another area in which I find a subtle difference between men and women is in giving bad news. This can be managing an individual who is not performing up to par, dealing with the realities of downsizing or layoffs, or informing employees that they are not going to get some expected recognition, such as an increase or promotion. Before IBM's downsizing in 1993, about 10 percent of the managers in my engineering/technical area were female. After the downsizing, I looked around, and it seemed the vast majority of the women had opted out of management. Perhaps the women had more difficulty than their male counterparts separating the business need to lay people off from the personal relationships they had developed with their employees. I observed a similar phenomenon in the early 2000s.

Managing poor performance is a critical aspect of leading and is every bit as important as rewarding and recognizing employees and teams. The latter is generally easy for women as they are natural team builders and cheerleaders, but the former can be more difficult. However, if someone is not pulling his or her weight, it drags the entire team down. People don't understand why you are tolerating the poor performance and frankly wonder why they should continue to work so hard. When a woman behaves like this, she is immediately labeled "too soft." If you go into management, having some training in managing difficult people and giving bad news is imperative.

Feedback is essential to success. People need feedback to understand what they do well and how they can improve. The more you can give credit when it's due (which women do very well) and provide feedback on deficiencies, including specific examples (which women can improve upon), the easier this will be. It is also very important to confront problems in a timely manner. Ignoring a performance issue implies you are accepting it. The longer you avoid the confrontation, the more entrenched the behavior becomes. Better to make your expectations known early and address issues before they become habits.

Feedback sessions are crucial to making sure your employees understand what they failed to do and also what steps they can take to improve. I have found another male-female difference here as well. Women often like to start by giving some positive feedback before getting to the meat of the issue. Be careful. This can backfire if the employees don't realize you are bringing them in to discuss some area where they fell short. Make sure you don't mix up your improvement sessions with too many compliments because you are afraid your employees will feel bad. Focus on the issues and the behaviors, not feelings. But listen to their reasons for having an issue before you pass judgment. (If you are going to be counseling an employee or working to improve a negative behavior, see the section on DMAIC in Chapter 7: I Can't Work with That Person.)

Even if you do everything right as a manager, you may encounter an employee who simply does not have the work ethic, desire, or ability to do the job. A good manager also needs to be able to decide when enough's enough and take appropriate action. It is not your failure if you have given your employee every opportunity to improve and he/she doesn't; it's his (or hers).

It is as important to consider managing "up" as to consider managing "down." By this I mean your relationship with the levels of management above you. Perhaps you can do your job with little direction and assistance from your bosses, but if you don't keep them informed of your issues and the problems (business, technical, or personnel) that you are resolving, you are selling both yourself and your employees short. How can senior managers know the excellent performance of your employees if you don't schedule periodic reviews with them, even if the news is all good? Then again, if it isn't, shouldn't you be keeping your management aware of any issues or surprises potentially coming? When performance ratings, salary increases, and other opportunities come along, the better the job you have done managing up, the better the outcome for your team and for yourself.

Try It Now
Are You Managing Up?

- Does your management chain know you?
- Does your management chain know your employees?
- Do you schedule reviews or opportunities for management to see your department's accomplishments?
- Can you promote, give increases, or otherwise reward your best employees without significant challenge from your management?

If the answers to any of the above questions is no, you need to focus more on managing upward in addition to managing your department.

As a leader in your company, you have another responsibility besides managing downward and upward, and that is preparing for the future. Again, you may be doing this with your business or technical projects, but how about organizationally? Who will be the next generation of leaders in your company if you are not preparing them? I consider it every leader's responsibility to be developing his or her replacement(s). This not only assures future success, but it also enables the leaders to move on to their next challenge while the business continues to perform. So who will replace you when you move to your next opportunity? If you can't answer that as a leader, then you aren't doing your job. And since there is still a shortage of women leaders, women have an even greater responsibility to do this.

Of course, there may be people who will say you got to where you are because you are a woman or you are the token woman. Ignore them. They are jealous. They will probably be working for you someday because they focus on why they didn't get promoted instead of what they need to do in order to get there. In one of my second-level assignments, my manager was a woman, and I had a woman manager working for me. (This only happened once in my entire 30-year career at IBM!) People made comments about it being "petticoat junction." Rather than get upset, we three women laughed and used the joke ourselves. When we didn't take it personally, they stopped making the wisecracks.

How do you measure and improve on your abilities as a leader and a manager? There are many tools to help you improve your management skills. The single most important is to listen and communicate often with your employees. The more they trust and understand your desire to help them succeed, the more they will feed you constructive input. Ask them if you should have stepped in on a given situation or whether you should have stepped back on another. If your employees are suggesting areas in which you can improve, why is that different from when they suggest business or technical improvements? Use this advice just as you would advice from a technical or business expert. Take the data, analyze it, see if it fits with what you think is the right next step, and move forward.

There are many feedback mechanisms for managers. Within IBM, the more formal tool was something we called an opinion survey in the early years and changed to a manager feedback survey in more recent ones. In an anonymous manner, employees answer a set of questions and are encouraged to comment both positively and negatively on their leader's performance. This is an excellent tool that you should welcome. It is important to solicit feedback from your employees and your manager on how you can improve in the areas identified. You can actually learn more from a difficult survey than a good one. If you are communicating regularly with your employees and have an open relationship, they won't wait for a formal survey to tell you. As a result, your actual survey will be much better.

I always remember Mayor Koch asking the people of New York City, "How am I doing?" There is no reason you can't ask your employees, your manager, and your peers the very same thing. If your company has no formal mechanism for feedback, try creating your own: a suggestion box outside your office, programs like 360-degree assessments, or even your own informal paper (or online) survey handed out and completed anonymously. Solicit feedback from as many sources as possible. Just as you search for technical and business data and trends, your management abilities can change as different environments and challenges arise, so keep the feedback paths open.

Women can have a harder time than men taking constructive criticism because we tend to internalize information. Whenever I find myself or someone else falling into such a trap, I remember a line from the movie *Moonstruck*. Cher slaps Nicholas Cage across the face when he declares his love, demanding he "snap out of it." If I find myself taking criticism personally, I remind myself to "snap out of it," and it helps. My younger daughter refers to these as reality checks.

Another thing that is very important to realize as a manager in a company is that you cannot be transparent. You have a responsibility to represent the company's policies and practices, and the senior management strategy, as your own. If an employee doesn't agree with a practice and you sympathize, indicating you would change it if you could, you are compromising both yourself and your company. In the short run you may be popular, but in the long run they will lose respect for you as will your management.

Try It Now
Are You a Transparent Manager?

- Do you:

    1. Tell your employees you would if only the company allowed it?
    2. Repeat company policy word for word rather than explain it in terms that help others recognize how it applies to their position or organization?
    3. Say one thing with your words and another with your actions?

- If the answer to any of these questions is yes, you need to rethink your role as a manager. Yes, transparency may make you more popular in the short term, but in the long run, it works against your company and against the overall morale of any area. If you don't believe it, can't change it, and can't espouse it as your belief, then get out of management.

As I stated earlier, I have always practiced the philosophy of "making the boss look good." As a manager, this is even more important. Whenever faced with a choice, I always tried to put myself in my boss's shoes and make the decision that would help him or her. Sometimes that was not necessarily the best decision for my specific area of responsibility, but if it was a better IBM solution, I always put the good of the organization above the good of my specific unit. Making your boss successful will lead to your ultimate success and also demonstrate that you understand the broader business environment.

Another important area that separates the managers from the true leaders is how they foster creativity and appropriate risk taking. A business cannot grow without changing, and with change comes risk. The arrogance of success is to think you can do the very same thing tomorrow that you do today and remain triumphant. If you shoot down ideas that are outside your sphere of comfort, you are killing off the roots of growth. Successful risk taking is a process in which you can learn more from failure than success. I am not advocating blind risk where you encourage foolhardy behavior, but good leaders encourage others to move outside their comfort zones once in while. You will make mistakes; everyone does. What matters is what and how you learn from them.

As you lead others, you only have so much ability to define your team members. You may not always have the best players, but it is up to you to get the best from every player. Lead by example, and keep listening and learning. I heard a famous conductor give a very telling comment in an interview. He said, "I became a great conductor when I realized that I didn't make a sound." As a leader, you accomplish great things by getting others to reach their full potential, and together you can create a great symphony or a successful business.

6

I WISH I HAD A WIFE

You can have it all, just not at the same time.
—*My mother*

One of the hardest decisions I had to make in my career was after my first child was born. I originally joined IBM in 1969 as the first woman engineer in an advanced manufacturing engineering group. (There was one other woman engineer in a similar group, but we never actually worked on anything together, and amazingly, we never really sought each other out.) There were a number of recent male engineering graduates who had started a year or so ahead of me and a large group of seasoned male engineers. After joining IBM, I immediately enrolled in a graduate work-study program that enabled me to pursue a master's degree. When I became pregnant some months later, I remember my cubicle mate being very nervous I would go into labor at work, and he made a point during my last month to find a lot of reasons to be in the lab or working elsewhere.

In 1970, IBM did not have all of the excellent work-life balance options that it does today. For the type of assignments I had, there was no practical way I could work part-time. Maternity leave was three months max. Not sure what I wanted to do, I arranged to take a one-year leave of absence—three months maternity and nine months educational to complete my master's degree. My management team was extremely helpful in providing these options and encouraged me to return when the year was completed. I did complete the master's, and when the time came to return, I decided I was not ready to go back to full-time work. I resigned from IBM and got a job teaching science in a local private school. I also taught at Vassar College, Marist College, and the local community college. All institutions were very flexible about the timing and schedules for my courses, so I could juggle my time to allow for pickup and drop-off at nursery school and other child-care concerns. I hired a wonderful woman during the school year to care for the children at her home. She became and still is like another grandmother to my children. After ten years of teaching part-time with both daughters in school, I went back to IBM, and the stories described in Chapter 1 began.

The decision to work full-time, work part-time, or stay home is a difficult one, and there is no right answer. You have to decide what works for you and your particular situation. For me, working part-time was the best of both worlds. Luckily, we could afford the drop in income. (After all, our mortgage was only $136 a month!) In the summer, I hired a babysitter from the neighborhood while I taught college from 8:00 AM to 10:30 AM. Since the girls were late sleepers, I'd get home from teaching just as they'd finished breakfast, and we'd have the whole day together. During the regular school year, I sometimes taught evening classes. I would have dinner ready and walk out the door, leaving my husband to watch the kids. (Yes, I did make dinner—see the discussion about guilt and supermom.) By teaching, I was able to stay technical and keep my skills honed while still being with my children during their preschool years. This worked for me, but I did put my ultimate career on hold and essentially lost out on ten years of benefits. I think I caught up, and I don't regret my decision, but the point is that it was not "free."

My sister did the opposite. She worked full-time at an extremely high-powered position in her firm when her daughter was young. She had a full-time babysitter in her home. When her daughter started school and her husband was established in a law firm, she decided to become a stay-at-home mom and never returned to her corporate career. I have friends and coworkers who left industry forever as soon as their first child was born; I know others who went back to full-time work almost immediately. It is common today for fathers to be the primary caregiver and for mothers to work. The point of all this is, it's really a decision only you and your partner can make based on your individual circumstances and preferences.

If you do decide to work either full- or part-time as you raise your family, know that it isn't easy. In fact, it's hard. Very hard. So resolve to keep moving forward, one foot in front of the other. And, be prepared to feel guilty. I used to tell people that my secret for being a working mother was "balancing the guilt." Let me explain. Children go through separation anxiety at different times of their lives. Sometimes I would drop one or both of the girls off at their caregiver's home, and they would cry. (This was more common when it was just one of them. I guess they felt safety in numbers). One awful morning my daughter went so far as to grab onto my pants and scream every time I tried to walk out the door. She wouldn't tell me what was wrong; she just cried. After about fifteen minutes of trying, I had to leave my screaming toddler. I felt terrible and drove to work in tears. My first act was to call the babysitter (there were no cell phones then) who informed me my daughter was playing happily and had been within two minutes of my leaving. The next day she went to the babysitters without a tear.

One of my friends described this as "turning the knife." She always felt her children did this to play on our emotions and get something they wanted later. Kids are clever, and they will work you, but it can also just be how they were feeling that morning. You *can't* prevent this, you *will* feel guilty when you leave them, and they *will* turn out fine—better than fine—anyway.

An interesting observation I made about separation anxiety was the difference between when I dropped my children off at the child care provider's home (they sometimes cried) and when my husband did (they *never* cried). So whenever possible, I got them ready and had my husband drop them off. I wouldn't even mention this except that my daughter had the same phenomenon occur when she started bringing her daughter to day care. Whenever Daddy dropped her off, she went in happily. When Mommy dropped her off, she sometimes cried. So if you find a difference in behavior in your children depending on whether Mommy or Daddy drops them off, try to have the one who doesn't see the crying do the majority of the drop-offs.

By the way, separation anxiety doesn't go away as your children get older; it just becomes more of a surprise. I still remember a fateful day when my younger daughter was starting third grade. Her sister was starting junior high and that bus came about ten minutes earlier than the elementary school bus. The third grader, who was very mature and levelheaded, insisted that she was old enough to handle those ten minutes alone without going to a babysitter or a neighbor's home in the morning. So being a good mother who wanted to allow my daughter to demonstrate her independence, I agreed. The first day of school I stayed home and had her pretend that I wasn't there. Her sister left, she finished her school preparations, and she went out to catch the bus. After the bus arrived, I left for work. The next day, I left at my normal time, which was before either bus arrived. About 8:30 AM I got a call from my younger daughter at home. She was hysterical. Trying to keep us both from panicking, I asked her, "Are you hurt?"

Her tearful answer, "No!"

I asked, "Did you miss the bus?"

Her tearful answer, "No."

"Are you afraid of something?" I asked.

Again a tearful, "No!"

Trying to stay calm I persisted, "So what's wrong?"

Her anguished response cut me to the quick, "I don't know, but I do know that if you were here, I wouldn't be crying."

Ugh. I was ready to rush home and take her to school but realized her bus would arrive before I could even get there. I calmly encouraged her to gather her stuff, go outside to the bus stop where the other children were already gathering, and she'd feel better. I told her I'd stay on the line until she left. She stopped crying and left the house a few minutes later. (It was still before cell phones, so I had to say good-bye before she went outside.) All day long I felt like the world's worst mother. I could barely stay focused on my meetings. Talk about guilt. How could I have just left my baby all alone like that? What kind of wicked witch mother was I? Promptly at 3:30 PM, the time she was due home from school, I called our house. She answered all bubbly and excited about her day. I asked her what the problem was in the morning and why she was so upset. At first she didn't even remember what I was talking about, and then when reminded, she brushed it off saying, "Oh, it was no big deal." I thought, "*No big deal!*" My entire day was ruined, and she'd forgotten all about it.

I tell this story (much to the chagrin of my daughter) because it points out several things. First, children can have separation anxiety at many different ages and often when a "first" occurs. Expect it. Next, in almost every case, a few minutes after you leave, the crying subsides, and your child will be happily engaged in whatever activity he/she is doing. Finally, you can't avoid feeling guilty. (By the way, the next morning my daughter again insisted she could handle being alone for the ten minutes, and she was fine from that day on.)

Another guilt source will occur when you have to miss an event in your child's life because something major in your career conflicts. I was in Japan when my younger daughter went to her first prom. Her dad did a great job taking lots of photos and having one of her friends come over so they could help each other get ready, but I missed the big event. You can be sure I was there for the prom the following year.

On the other side, when you have to stay home with a sick child and miss an important work activity or have to ask someone to handle some items for you that can't wait, you will feel guilty. Again, my advice is to be kind to yourself. Know that it's okay to be with your sick child and not on your computer/ PDA/phone at every chance. Know that when things are going smoothly, you do more than your fair share, and on balance it'll work. You will feel guilty that you don't have enough time for your husband, so you will try to get all kinds of tasks done in your spare time like shopping/cleaning/cooking/ whatever. And when your husband pitches in, as he should, you may also feel guilty because we were brought up expecting this to be women's work. My daughters tell me this is no longer true, that they expect their husbands to do just as much as they do, but I'm not convinced.

All this will pull at you in different ways at different times. I have no magic solution other than to try to "balance the guilt." It is perfectly all right to feel guilty. I have found some women even feel guilty about feeling guilty which, frankly, is absurd. I consider feeling guilty a sign that you care.

One of my friends likes to get together with other working moms and share "bad mommy" stories. In these sessions, they share stories about how their hectic lives caused them to let their children down, like forgetting to send lunch to daycare or forgetting to get valentine cards when every other child had them to hand out. She claims these sessions make them feel a little more normal, to know they are not alone. I'm not sure about the stories, but getting together with other working parents has many benefits: you are doing something for yourself, you realize your situation is not unique, you will often learn tips from each other, and you can back each other up for babysitting or emergencies.

As you try to balance all of these guilt sources, the thing that will give is your time. It's very common to want to prove to yourself and to the world that you can do it all. As such, you try to be supermom, superwife, superemployee, superfriend; but what you really become is superexhausted. You need some "me" time for whatever it is that makes you feel special. Schedule it and make it happen. Get help if you can afford it: someone to clean your house, take-out meals, a babysitter in the evening, whatever works. If the quantity of time you have is short, then make the quality high by spending meaningful time with your children and family. (More on this later in the chapter as we discuss how to organize your chaotic life.)

My "me" time was reading. I would get engrossed in a novel and my concentration was so intense, I could tune everyone out. Of course, that drove my family a little crazy as they would talk to me and I wouldn't hear them. My daughters found a solution. Whenever they wanted my attention they would yell, "Mom, your hair's on fire," and I would finally look up.

This guilt complex is something my younger daughter and I have debated, as she is now a working mom. She feels guilt but doesn't *want* to feel guilty. She doesn't *want* to balance it but wants to come up with a way not to feel it at all. Or, to feel it and move on. Balancing the guilt was my way of accepting the fact that I can't help what I feel, but I can rationalize why I feel that way.

Another question I hear a lot from working mothers is about the long-term effects of working on their children. My mother worked full-time from the day I started kindergarten. I worked part-time shortly after my daughters were born and then full-time as soon as they started school. We all turned out okay. In fact, I think working helped my children learn independence. Both my daughters went back to work shortly after the birth of their first child. As more of my coworkers' children are going into the working world, I have found many of their daughters also returning to work after having their children. There is no "right answer". Find the solution that works for you, knowing it may change as your children mature, your finances change and your job progresses.

When my younger daughter was in high school, she took part in a debate during social studies class on whether mothers should work. I was gratified to see that she took the side of the working mother, arguing all the advantages. During this debate, her opponent, trying to bring the point closer to home, countered that my daughter had never had the pleasure of eating a homemade apple pie. My daughter was a bit taken aback by that comment, but quickly recovered with arguments that there were more important and less fattening things than homemade apple pie. Her friends found the argument amusing. The next day in class, they presented her with a purchased apple pie, taping over the name on the box from Mrs. Smith's Apple Pie to read Mrs. Weisman's Apple Pie. She proudly brought it home for dinner, and we all shared a good laugh (and a slice of pie).

Other decisions you may have to make include whether to bring your child (or children) to daycare or to arrange for care at home. If at home, do you choose a daily sitter or a live-in nanny? There are advantages and disadvantages on both sides, and again there is no right answer. Whatever you choose, there are many considerations. Obviously a live-in nanny who has impeccable credentials leaves you with the most flexibility. Child care at an established and well-credentialed institution provides your child with socialization and professional care. Consider the financial implications of each, the ease with which you can get your children going in the morning, whether it bothers you to come home to a house that might look very different (messy) than when you left, your children's age, and most importantly, the quality of the caregiver. I preferred a private woman caring for my children in her home. Some of the advantages for me were that not being a "day care," she only watched a few children and the colds/infections that children often pick up at day care were reduced. In addition, if she had no one else on a particular day and one of the kids was sick, she often was willing to come to our house. Finally, she was in the same school district, so I could have the kids take the school bus to her house after school and not need to arrange special driving midday. On the other hand, my granddaughter and grandson attend an amazing day care institution that they love and at which they thrive. And for their parents who may experience separation anxiety, the school has a web cam going all day so parents (and grandparents) can watch their children from their computers throughout the day,

In any case, you need to also have a backup plan in case your child is sick or the primary caregiver is sick. My husband and I would often split the day when one child was sick—I, taking the morning and he, taking the afternoon, or vice versa. In addition, we had lined up some relatives and friends whom we could call in a crisis.

Other things to consider include what you can afford, your child's age, and number of siblings; do you need to get your child to other activities before or after the care, does your child have special needs, and more. Many companies offer child care consulting or even in-house child care. Whichever route you take, get references and check them out. Stop in unexpectedly once in a while if your child is too young to tell you about his or her day. If your day care center has a web cam, check in periodically during the day.

No matter what path you choose, make sure you make the most of the time you have with your young family because before you know it, your children will grow and have their own friends and need their private time.

It is hard to separate work and home when there is a pressing problem at either location, but when everything is normal, try to establish some boundaries. In general, I always needed some decompression time. During most of my career, I worked about twenty-five minutes from home. During the drive in, I would think about my day and organize some of the key things I wanted to accomplish in my head during that time. By the time I arrived at work, I was in "work mode." When I left for home, the same thing happened in reverse. I focused on the evening ahead and what I wanted to do with my family, and by the time I arrived, I was in "family mode."

In the early days we weren't as "connected," so it was easier to keep the two worlds apart unless there was an emergency. As we got home terminals, then modems, and now wireless anywhere, some of that separation has blurred. This is not necessarily a good thing. My advice in today's highly connected world is to try to not log on at all until the kids are in bed, you have spent meaningful time with your partner, and you have finished whatever you wanted to do at home. (A friend of mine calls this establishing a personal firewall, just as your computer has a firewall to protect from spam and unwanted e-mails. I like this analogy.) Log on only if doing that will lighten the load for the next day. If not, all you are doing is chaining yourself to work for that much longer a day. However, if your older children are doing their homework, you become an excellent role model for them to see you doing work each night. When I taught, I'd work on lesson plans each night, and the girls and I frequently sat down together to all do "our" homework. Try not to become a slave to your home computer or PDA—block out a maximum amount of time and don't do it at all unless it helps you free up time later.

Another advantage of today's wired and wireless world is the ease with which many employees can work from home. Best Buy has a program that allows employees to work on whatever schedule best fits their life. Many IBM locations have unique diversity programs to compete in the war for talent. They support considerable working from home, day care centers set up near the workplace, and other solutions to help working families. Not every job allows for this, but if you can find one that offers this type of flexibility, you get the best of both worlds. I never had the opportunity to do this while my children were living at home, although in the latter years of my career I did take the opportunity to work from home when I had a day of remote meetings. Instant messaging, Net meetings, wireless, teleconferences, and team rooms help us work from almost anywhere, again a good and bad thing.

There are some great advantages to working from home—you save commute time and you can pop something in the oven while you are waiting for a call, throw in a load of laundry or start dinner. (We women are great at multitasking.) But in general, I find it best to operate at home just like in the office.

Renee's Rules
for Working from Home

- Have a home office where you won't be distracted.
- Have another caregiver present as you cannot watch your children and do your job at the same time. If possible, don't tell your kids you are home, so they can't interrupt you.
- Get up and walk around after each meeting or phone call and at least every hour.
- Keep work in the office, and home in the rest of the house. (Of course, if it's a beautiful day and you want to work from your sunporch and noone will disturb you there, why not?)
- Make a point of getting into the main office periodically to be seen, meet others, and stay in touch.
- Above all, set working hours. Remember that working from home does not mean that your workday never ends!

No matter what path you choose, there will be times when it seems to all pile up. I remember having a particularly harried day with one of my toddler daughters and complaining to a parent of older children that it'd be so much easier when she grows up. The parent smiled at me and said, very seriously, "My dear, it doesn't get better, it just gets different." I remembered that often as the problems and issues my teenaged, college-aged, and now adult daughters experienced were indeed "different." Another friend liked to remind me, "Little children, little problems. Big children, big problems."

When it does pile up and seem like too much, ask for help. One day a young coworker came to me with tears in her eyes. The night before, her one-year-old son was ill and woke up crying multiple times.

After a sleepless night, she had to leave the baby with her husband so she could get in early to give a major presentation to a very senior executive. She had worked on and obsessed over the presentation for weeks. When she got in, apparently there was some pressing issue that caused the executive to cancel the meeting. She was devastated and ready to pack it all in. I calmed her down, listened, empathized, and helped her realize that she needed to "get away from it all" for a little while and encouraged her to spend the rest of the day doing something just for her. These experiences and frustrations happen to all of us; but the more tired, worried, and guilty we are feeling, the more magnified they become in our mind. This is when you have to take a reality check—and take care of yourself first. If you can't spare an entire day, then take a walk, go exercise, sit with your feet up and sip a latte, or find some other means to get away for even a little while.

Whenever you find it (work/life/kids/relationship/whatever) is getting too intense, get some help: your partner, parents, friends, babysitters, counselors, whomever. When that all-encompassing pressure starts to consume you, you need an escape valve. Unfortunately, many women find it easier to do something nice for others than for themselves. Make a list of the things that give you pleasure and reward yourself by scheduling the time to do them. You cannot be effective if you are burnt out, run-down, or upset.

It is important to find ways to prioritize. I often reminded myself, "Don't sweat the small stuff." There are times you simply have to say no, be it at home, with your child, at work, or with outside commitments. You can do many things, and women are masters at juggling many tasks, but do the ones that matter. You need private time, whatever that means to you. You will also continually reprioritize, on a weekly or even daily basis. There are questions I ask myself to help put things in perspective: Will that issue still be there tomorrow? Will it really matter in a month? In ten years? Will I be of more benefit to myself and others if I do it or leave it? This may help you decide what can wait and what needs attention now.

Additional tips I have learned from other women who have successfully prioritized their lives include having a heart-to-heart with your life partner to really split the responsibilities. Another interesting concept came from a manager who regularly scheduled "one-on-ones" with each of her employees to make sure she stayed on top of their projects and concerns. She decided to do the same with her family. She scheduled one hour of one-on-one time with each member of her family each week to focus on whatever they wanted to do. Others scheduled "alone" time to assure they had time for themselves. I never really utilized either of these, but I do know this has worked well for many people.

Whenever you can work it out, try to take the less-important tasks and either postpone them or have someone else perform them for you. Rachel Ray may have thirty-minute meals, but some of mine took even less than that. On the other hand, sometimes I welcomed housework or cooking as it made me feel like I had accomplished something and used a different part of my brain. A young working mother in my organization once said, "You have to make the time because it won't make itself."

It is said that in real estate only three things matter: location, location, and location. To succeed in work-life balancing only three things matter: organization, organization, and organization. There are many little steps you can take to add organization back to your chaotic life.

Renee's Rules
*for Using Electronic Messaging
Without It Controlling You!*

- Unless you are required to have twenty-four-hour, seven-day-a-week access, turn your computer, PDA, and/or business phone off for some period of time every day and get away from it all. Find some "me" time.
- Unless it will save you time another day or someone is expecting information from you, don't log on outside of working hours. If it does save you time, then do it but be sure you are not just adding to your workload so you have more time during the day to take on more.
- Your e-mail is not your "to do" list. When you read an e-mail, practice the 4 Ds:

  1. Delete it.
  2. Do it.
  3. Delegate it.
  4. Defer it (this should be the smallest group).

- Unless it is in the defer category, you shouldn't have to handle the e-mail again. The same rules should apply to snail mail and snail memos if you still receive any.

When my girls were young, I'd lay out their clothes for school and get their lunches ready the night before. This shortened the morning hassle. I made lists for everyone by day so we all knew who had to be where by when. I used to espouse the energy versus entropy theory to my family whenever they let things get out of hand. As a chemist, the second law of thermodynamics states that the entropy (disorder) of the universe naturally increases. The greater the disorder, the greater the energy it takes to remove that disorder. I turned this into a life lesson. If you do a little every day, the task never gets that big, be it laundry or cleaning or homework. In effect, the energy to do it is lessened. Also, you delegate at work, what's wrong with doing it at home? Giving your family jobs to do helps a lot. As my girls got older, they were completely in charge of the laundry. My husband handled all the outdoor tasks, and we often brought dinner in or went out to eat. I have a friend who assigned one meal a week to each family member. Her husband was responsible for Monday dinner, her teenage daughter for Tuesday, and her teenage son for Wednesday. Dinner could be elaborate or take-out, but it was up to the responsible person to handle it. It was amazing how quickly her family came to appreciate planning ahead.

Renee's Rules
for Getting Out the Door with Two Kids and Other Favorite Timesavers

- Prepare whatever you can the night before (lunches, coats, clothes, special items needed for school, anything you need to take to work), and leave them by the door or put them in the car when possible.
- Keep extras in the car (kids' bottles, diapers, clothes, underwear, favorite blanket, sweater, jacket, etc.).
- Keep lists handy and visible—who has to be where, what you need to buy, which errands need to be run, and who is doing what.
- Do whatever you can online—paying bills or personal shopping takes less time online and may even be cheaper.
- Keep stuff where you use it (lunchboxes near fridge, hamper near where kids take clothes off, etc.).
- Barbeque whenever possible. (In my case, my husband would do it, and the kitchen would stay cleaner!)
- Clean as you go and train your family to do the same (wishful thinking, but sometimes it works).

Many women fall into the trap of doing the household tasks because they don't like the way their husbands do it. Come on now—that is the ultimate control issue. Your husband *can* learn which pants can't go in the dryer or how to keep dark clothes from white. Not giving up the task because you do it better is something he will certainly allow you to continue doing, but you are putting the extra work on yourself!

Time-management training teaches you to keep track of your schedule for an entire week in order to analyze what you are doing with your time. You then review what you can eliminate, what you can do at the same time, what is absolutely critical, etc. While this is more rigor than I have ever practiced outside of work, having a planner or PDA with all your professional and personal information in one place is a necessity. It is also helpful to have everyone's calendar (yours, your husband's, and your children's) integrated in one place, especially for after-work times. Your PDA, cell phone, and computer most likely have an alarm that you can use to remind yourself of commitments. I have also set an alarm to ring so I can graciously exit a phone call or a meeting with someone who just loves to talk and eat up your time. To-do lists, if you are disciplined enough to create them and check off as you complete, are excellent to help you remember and prioritize.

One activity that can help you get organized is creating an activity log.

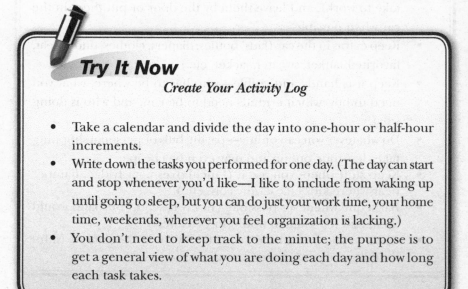

Try It Now
Create Your Activity Log

- Take a calendar and divide the day into one-hour or half-hour increments.
- Write down the tasks you performed for one day. (The day can start and stop whenever you'd like—I like to include from waking up until going to sleep, but you can do just your work time, your home time, weekends, wherever you feel organization is lacking.)
- You don't need to keep track to the minute; the purpose is to get a general view of what you are doing each day and how long each task takes.

Now that you have created the log over whatever period makes sense to you, the next step is to analyze it for opportunities.

Try It Now

Analyze Your Activity Log

After you have completed your activity log, go through and mark the items that are top priority with a yellow highlighter. Mark the items that are low priority with a blue highlighter. Mark the items that are specifically for *you* with a pink highlighter (assuming you had any, which many women don't).

Now answer these questions about your activities:

1. Are any tasks unnecessary?
2. Am I spending more time on low-priority tasks than high-priority ones?
3. Are there any activities that could be eliminated? Postponed? Given to someone else? Done concurrently?
4. Am I doing the hardest jobs when my energy level is highest? (I am a morning person, so I can get difficult tasks out of the way much faster early in the day versus nearer bedtime.) Are you doing them in the best place? (I am inspired by sunlight, so if I wrote this book on my sun porch, it flowed much more easily than when I worked in a darker office.)
5. Can I do any of these tasks more efficiently?
6. Am I repeating something several times that would be better done once or vice versa?
7. Am I taking any time just for me?

This technique, when used periodically, can help you organize. Invoke it when you find your stress level starting to go up, and you think you just can't keep up the pace any longer. It also can help you look for things you might do to save time by organizing better. Another method for prioritizing is to classify your to-do list into *urgent, important, not urgent,* and *not important.* If you have trouble deciding which items to color blue and yellow above, this may help. Work on the urgent and important tasks first and skip the not urgent, not important ones.

The bibliography includes some Web sites with additional tips for time management.

Hopefully some of these tricks will help you find some time for the things you personally love to do. Work-life balance means you need a life, too.

If something is important to you, find the time to do it. When I decided to write this book, I knew it was going to be a lengthy undertaking and consume a huge amount of time. So I took steps to find and make that time. First, I made it a goal, both career and personal. I used the time when I was most productive (early morning) and blocked out all distractions while I wrote (turned off email and IM, used caller ID to decide whether to answer phone, worked in my inspiring sunny office). I just wrote, without editing, until I was done. For each chapter, I began with two pages to decide what I was going to share (see the Say it in a Few Words exercise in Chapter 4). I complimented myself when I finished each day. It took three years, but I did it.

I received a valuable piece of advance about balancing my work and home life early in my career. During a particular technical crisis my manager saw me getting frustrated over working late and told me to go home. His advice was, "Get the job done and do it well, but don't let the company own your happiness." His point, and it was sage advice, was that throughout your career there will be ups and downs. Sometimes you will be in a situation that no matter how hard or cleverly you work, you can't prevent an issue that might have a negative effect on your career. If you have wrapped your happiness up in career advancement, you will be setting yourself up to be devastated when this problem hits. If on the other hand, you have balance and your happiness comes from both inside and outside work, then when these setbacks occur, you will roll with the punches. Finding that balance between work and home will make you better at both.

When my daughter was pregnant with her first child, she asked the global leader of her business, a mom with two grown kids, how she did it—how she had it all. She said two important things (and they just happened to be exactly what my daughter needed to hear):

1. Leave at 5:00 PM. Don't worry about perception. Go spend time with your family. And if you need to do work after they go to bed, so be it. But enjoy your family. Your work and accomplishments will still be noticed.
2. Vacations are vacations. Don't take your computer or PDA. You need time to reconnect with your family, to refresh, and to recharge.

My daughter followed her advice, reminding herself "don't worry about perception" as she ran out every night to catch the 5:31 train (and once in awhile even the 5:01 train!). She spent a few hours with her family, put her daughter to bed, and then logged back on. And she was promoted the next year—even with "leaving" at 5:00. Don't worry about perception—it's results that matter.

I had a friend in another company who did not practice this advice. She worked all the time, putting her personal life a far second to her career. She rarely saw her fiancé and kept postponing setting a date for the wedding because she was "too busy." She would work all day at work, go home, eat dinner while doing her e-mail, and then proceed to work late into the evening. Besides burning herself out, she lost her objectivity. She got into a very damaging situation at work. Rather than advancing for all the hours and exhausting effort she had expended, she ended up leaving the company. She let work own her happiness, and it wasn't until she left that she reestablished balance. Today she is happily married, working elsewhere (still very hard), but when she goes home, she goes home.

Another young woman that I encountered in external coaching was in a similar position. She had taken a job as a manager in an extremely hectic area where the workload far exceeded the number of people to handle it. She was new in management and less experienced at delegating. She was somewhat of a perfectionist, and as a result, she worked long hours and every weekend. She ended up with high blood pressure and other health issues. Perhaps this was not caused by her stress level, but I cannot help but think it was at least a factor. She finally agreed she was burning herself out and went to her boss, expecting to hear that she was copping out. Instead, her boss indicated that he had seen this coming, did not want to lose her from the company, and would do whatever possible to find her a position that would enable her to get her personal health and balance back in order.

I tell this story for several reasons. First, this individual had let her job own her happiness and, as a result, could not get back in balance. Just as significant was the fact that the young woman was actually surprised to hear that she was doing such an excellent job, and her dedication was recognized. That fact alone lifted a huge weight off of her shoulders! She did not appreciate her own worth and never thought to negotiate herself out of that oppressive position until it became a health crisis. I have seen other men and women put their family situations in jeopardy because of work demands. This chapter is about balance, and it is one of the most important elements of your career. Make sure you reassess your balance periodically and if you are too far one way or the other, re-balance.

By the way, colleagues will sometimes make comments about the time you are away from the office, and surprisingly, I found many women to be worse than men. You just have to be thick-skinned. Remember, you are balancing two worlds, while Atlas only had one on his back.

Even if you are an expert at balance, there will be times when no matter what you do, you will question your decisions. When that happens, I remember a comment my mother used to say when people asked her whether she worried that her working would have a negative effect on her children. Mom would answer, "If you love your children, they will know it whether you work at home or not, and my children know how much I love them." Yes, we certainly did, Mom, and I believe my daughters knew (and know) how much I love them, too.

7

I CAN'T WORK WITH
THAT PERSON

Men of quality are not threatened by women seeking equality.
—Unknown

Throughout your career, you will deal with a number of difficult coworkers, employees, or bosses who will affect your ability to do your job. In all cases, common sense, a stiff upper lip, and a systematic logical approach to the difficult person will normally bring the situation back under control. Easier said than done, but in this chapter I will share some basic techniques I have used successfully to address these situations. Like anything else, practice makes perfect.

There appear to be two distinct schools of thought as to how women should "act" when confronted with difficult people in the business environment. I have seen many books encouraging women not to change their behaviors but to remain "nice." I have also seen many encouraging women to become more assertive and aggressive to keep others from taking advantage of them. So who is right? Actually, they both are, depending on the situation and the type of difficult individual with whom you are dealing. Just as situational leadership advises you to change your style depending on how willing and capable your employees may be, you need to change your style depending on how irrational and pointed the difficult individuals are.

Regardless of the situation, you need to take action, or the situation will never change. The longer you wait, the more you are condoning the behavior. If you don't deal with it, it will more than likely continue. Moreover, you will end up having to deal with it sooner or later.

In most cases, I have found women tolerate difficult situations longer than men do. As such, using some of the techniques in this chapter can help you do a reality check to determine if you should or should not confront.

Most people have personality traits that affect how easily you can work with them on a day-to-day basis. They may be outgoing or introverted, aggressive or docile, egocentric or insecure, forthcoming or closemouthed, etc. However, when these types are experiencing high levels of stress, their personalities can become even more extreme. The stress can come from an internal or an external source. Understanding the source of that stress can help to ensure you are addressing the real problem.

In addition, you may experience these difficulties with coworkers, employees, or management. How you confront can differ depending on where you are in that hierarchy. Difficult people can be male or female, and gender differences may or may not play a role in the particular situation. Moreover, the issues can occur in public or in private. They may need to be addressed immediately, or it may be better to wait until everyone has cooled off. With all these things to consider, how can you know what to do? In reality, it is much simpler than you think, once you have learned to recognize the types and get practice in confronting problems.

This chapter will describe two distinct types of situations you may experience in confronting people, with examples of how to handle both. First, it looks at chronic problems where you have time to apply a structured scientific approach. Then it will cover acute situations that occur when a particular individual may attack, undermine, or otherwise surprise you, and you need to respond immediately. Knowing what to say and how to say it can quickly bring the situation back under control.

My first rule for successful confrontations is to recognize that there is only one person you can really control, yourself. The solution starts with you. Don't allow yourself to get roped in or emotionally upset. Stay objective and approach the situation as a fact-finding mission.

Let's begin with a few basics about conflict management. In their book *Crucial Confrontations*, Patterson et al. discuss applying CPR—content, pattern, and relationship—to determine if you should confront an issue. The following summarizes their approach, and I have found it to be an excellent reality check. As a woman who was somewhat hesitant to "make waves," this process helped me realize when to step up to an issue.

Essentially, they recommend you start by stating or writing down exactly what the problem is. Then, look for a pattern. Is it a habitual issue, or is the person just having a bad day? Finally, consider the problem in relationship to you and others. Is it something that is impacting your ability to do your job or those of the people around you? Is it creating an unpleasant environment? If the answer to these questions is yes, you must take action. (If the answer is no, then your next question should be to yourself. Is the problem the person or you? And if you are the problem, you need to understand what is really bothering you before you act. Have you ever gotten into a disagreement with someone and somewhere in the middle asked yourself, why are we arguing about this? If so, you probably neglected to perform CPR first.)

Once you decide you need to confront the individual, you must spend time preparing for that discussion. I am a scientist, so I like to start with basic scientific principles. I have found that the very same techniques I use when attacking a technical problem are just as effective with people problems. As an engineer, I was trained in an approach called DMAIC, which is part of six sigma and lean concepts. It is a structured method I have used often to solve technical problems. I decided to try it when I encountered a problem with a difficult coworker, and I found that this step by step, objective process actually helped solve the issue. I have used it many times since with similar results.

The DMAIC process is very simple. When you have a problem, you first need to *define* it. Then you *measure* it, *analyze* the data, take steps to *improve* it, and monitor those changes to make sure the problem is under *control*. With a personnel or behavior problem, I modify it ever so slightly as in the table below.

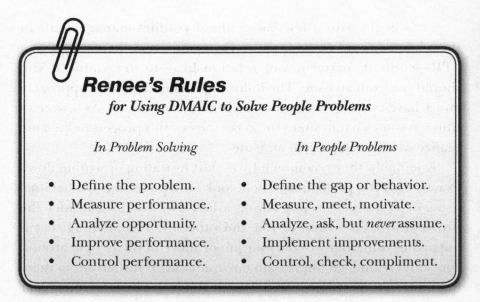

Renee's Rules
for Using DMAIC to Solve People Problems

In Problem Solving	In People Problems
• Define the problem.	• Define the gap or behavior.
• Measure performance.	• Measure, meet, motivate.
• Analyze opportunity.	• Analyze, ask, but *never* assume.
• Improve performance.	• Implement improvements.
• Control performance.	• Control, check, compliment.

Some of the first steps of this approach overlap with what you did in CPR, but they are now targeted toward taking action as opposed to deciding if you should. Since the process is so structured, let's take each section in turn.

Try It Now
How to Apply DMAIC to People Problems

- Define the problem.

  1. What specific behaviors have you observed?
  2. What is the difference (gap) between how the person is acting and the behavior you would like to see?

- Measure the problem.

  1. When does it occur?
  2. How often does it occur?
  3. *The more specific you can be here, the better.*

- Analyze the situation.

  1. What would you like to happen differently?
  2. What don't you know about why this behavior is occurring?
  3. What types of words would you use to describe this in a non-threatening way?
  4. What is the worst that can happen, and what would you do if that occurred? What is the best outcome?
  5. *Role-play whenever possible before meeting with the individual.*

- Implement.

  1. Schedule the discussion or meeting with the person.
  2. Decide how you will start the discussion.
  3. Begin with non-threatening remarks.
  4. Explain why you want to talk.
  5. Ask the right questions.

- Control and compliment.

  1. After the meeting, be sure to follow up.
  2. Document the discussion.
  3. Compliment the person when the behavior improves

Always start by defining what the behavior or issue is. Focus on what you have observed and seen, not rumor or innuendo. Do not try to solve at this point. And don't try to guess or, worse, assume why the behavior is occurring.

The next step is to measure the problem. Is it happening often? What is its effect on you? What is its effect on others? What is its effect on the business?

Is there any trigger that precipitates the behavior? Do certain situations bring it out? Think about objections and reactions the person might have. I also ask myself, "What is the worst thing that can happen if I bring this up?" And try to prepare for that.

If you are very uncomfortable about addressing the individual, role-play with someone in advance. This could be another manager, someone from human resources, or someone who does not know the individual. I do not suggest role-playing with another employee.

When you have your description of the issue and its impacts clearly defined, schedule the discussion. The meeting should occur in a private place with just the two of you. Choose a location where you won't be disturbed or interrupted. Other people present may be perceived as "ganging up" by the person you want to confront. If you have any reason to believe the person may become belligerent or threatening, make sure that while your discussion is private, others are not faraway and sit closer to the exit than the person you are confronting.

Start by putting the person at ease and state your issue in a non-threatening manner. If the individual feels threatened or defensive, you will not get to the heart of the problem. (I once had a coworker enter my office with the comment, "I could kill you." That certainly didn't start off the conversation well.)

I like to start the discussion with a statement of the issue followed by a non-threatening question. Some examples include:

- "You promised to have the _____ ready yesterday, and I did not get it. What happened?"
- "This morning you were very upset when I asked you to take on this new project. Can you explain what the problem was?"
- "You have been late to our last three staff meetings. Is there a problem that prevents you from getting here on time?"

Use examples and data whenever possible. Focus on the behaviors you have observed. Accept that you can't really change the person's personality, but you can affect his or her actions and behaviors as they affect you. If possible, show how doing what you suggest will help him/her and the business. The more you can focus the discussions on the business and business results, the more impartial and effective you will be. Agree on the next steps and define a time to follow up. Documenting the discussion is critical to ensuring you both understand what was agreed to.

Okay, so now we have the steps defined. How do we customize these steps to match the behavior to the type? DMAIC is a process, but it doesn't have all of the answers. But by forcing you to ask the right questions, it keeps you focused on the issues and correcting them. The best way to demonstrate its versatility is through examples. Please note that the names of the following individuals have been changed (to protect the innocent?).

Egotists can be very threatening types for a newly initiated female. These people are usually highly competent, focused on getting things done, and often don't care about how. They love to monopolize meetings or make threatening remarks in your meetings. They are often in positions of authority and use that authority to further their ego.

I once had a fifth-line manager, Al, who for me represented a typical egotist. This was in my early years with IBM, and it has been a long time since I have seen this kind of behavior. However, I am sure there are companies where Als still exist. Al relished the opportunity to lecture people on just how smart he was. He frequently reminded you that if you didn't like the way he was doing things, you could either leave the organization or he'd fire you. For me, one of his most annoying traits was to single me out in meetings. Picture a room full of fifteen male managers and one female (me). Al would frequently go off on a tirade about some item. For effect, he would usually use some sort of four-letter word. However, he did not want to swear in front of me, so before he used the four-letter word, he'd apologize to me in advance. A typical remark would be something like, "If people don't, excuse me, Renee, f—ing like that, they can leave," or "Tell him he's now on my, excuse me, Renee, s—t list," or other such comments. I have to ask if he had enough presence of mind to recognize the word was inappropriate and apologize, then couldn't he have picked another word? But if not, why single me out? By singling me out, he somehow implied that I should be treated differently.

At one such meeting, another middle manager asked Al why he only apologized to me, saying, "Don't you think we might also find it offensive?" I wanted to thank that individual for his support, but at the same time, it was not the right thing to do. Embarrassing Al in front of others was not something he appreciated, and that manager was now on Al's "s—t list."

So what should you do when you encounter an Al? Let's walk through the steps we identified. First of all, apply CPR. What was the content? Al was singling me out as woman. Was it habitual? Yes. What was our relationship, and was this affecting my ability to perform? Not really, but his continual occurrence annoyed me and had an effect on others as well.

Second, consider DMAIC. My definition of the gap was that Al treated me differently, and I measured this regularly when he went on a tirade. In the analysis phase, I realized if it had only been me, I might not have stepped forward, but he had a negative effect on coworkers; therefore, I could not ignore the behavior. I decided to improve the situation by setting up a private meeting with Al. This privacy was critical—never ever embarrass your boss in front of others. At this meeting, I told Al how uncomfortable he made me, not because he was swearing, but because he was treating me differently from every other member of the team. If he felt he had to swear, just do it. I'd heard the words before and even used them once in a while. In this meeting I was nice but reminded him that women did not like to be treated differently. (The implicit threat being that he was not being equitable to women.) I think this may have been the first time a woman ever brought forward an issue to him, and frankly, Al was taken aback. He actually thought he was doing the right thing by apologizing first. After the meeting, Al not only stopped apologizing but more often than not, stopped swearing as well. Of course, every so often Al reverted to type, but it was the exception now rather than the rule. No further follow-up was necessary. I had made my point. By bringing this to him privately and in a very unemotional manner, Al heard me, and he did make some attempt to change. He appreciated the feedback, and unlike my coworker, I didn't end up on his bad side.

My second example involves a colleague. Jack tried to get along with everyone and to avoid confrontation. Initially I liked Jack a lot. He always understood just what I was concerned about, and whenever I couldn't resolve something, Jack empathized greatly, blaming the "system." I felt like he really understood me, but eventually I realized he agreed with everyone on every position. As such, whenever we had to escalate an issue or convince others of our point of view, he was wishy-washy, ineffectual, and often switched positions during the meeting. Applying CPR, I realized that the issue with Jack was he could not stand firm on any position. In fact, he was really patronizing. It certainly was a pattern, and it affected my relationship with him to the point that I had to take appropriate steps. However, I realized that confronting Jack would be ineffectual because he would agree with me. So what could I do?

Taking each step of DMAIC, the problem was that Jack's continual inability to hold a position left issues directionless. Because I worked with Jack, I did not want our team to be negatively impacted. After analyzing the problem, I realized that the best approach was to work "around" him, copying both him and his boss on many of my memos. I also made sure technical, business, or personnel information didn't stop in Jack's office by scheduling regular reviews with upper management under the premise of "employee visibility" and "opportunity for management to know the key contributors." This greatly improved the decision making since Jack agreed with his boss (who could make a decision and stick with it). Essentially, I controlled the situation by communicating beyond Jack.

There are other more subtle behaviors patronizing people may have, even though I did not find these with Jack. They may praise their employees and make them feel appreciated but in reality withhold opportunities, raises, and promotions. Or in a more subtle form of gender discrimination, they may withhold the resources that help bring about a female's success while providing them to male employees. This type of discrimination is much harder to identify, and the individuals may not even realize they are doing it. If you find your manager is often telling you what a good job you are doing while never really providing you with recommendations for improvement, but is giving the choice assignments and key budget and resource opportunities to another (male), your antenna should go up. In Chapter 6, I discuss goal setting and benchmarking yourself against a comparable male. This is a good technique to help you consider whether your boss is patronizing you. My advice in these cases is to keep a clear record of the accomplishments on which they are lavishing praise, question whether there are areas you need to improve upon, and specifically ask for the resources, budgets, or support you need to be successful. Patronizers are particularly dangerous to work for because you think they're in your corner, and frankly, so do they; but in reality, they are holding you back. They are so entrenched in this behavior that they don't even realize they are doing it.

The DMAIC process helped me deal with another coworker. George loved to talk and made judgments quickly. George had a great deal of trouble pronouncing my name. (I have actually found that people who don't bother to learn how to pronounce my slightly unusual name after repeated corrections are giving me a signal that they don't care about what I have to say.) George must have called me every name that started with *R*, from Rainey to Ronnie and, after many tries, settled on Rinney. No matter how often I corrected him, he would inevitably mess up the pronunciation. I even tried spelling my name phonetically for him a few times. Every time George spoke to me, he used a different incorrect pronunciation, so much so that others in the team started correcting him. This was before the days that I had read about CPR, but the pattern was so habitual that I finally became exasperated and knew I had to do something.

After applying DMAIC and recognizing the problem was that George's ears were smaller than his mouth, I decided the best approach was not a meeting but a more drastic and somewhat humorous approach. I started calling him "Geoff." After a few times of hearing himself referred to as Geoff, he reminded me his name was George, not Geoff. I told him my name wasn't Rinney either. He looked at me strangely and asked, "You mean you don't like being called Rinney?" I sweetly responded, "Not any more than you like being called Geoff." He countered, "But Geoff isn't my name!" I answered, again quite matter-of-factly, "And Rinney isn't mine." From that day on, he pronounced my name right.

This might have been a bit extreme, but it was very effective. He and I laughed about it from time to time and even purposely used Geoff and Rinney when we wanted to make some sort of point with each other. My point with this is, try to interject some humor now and then when you feel people aren't listening. It need not be this pointed, but it can be effective. The solution came to me because I spent the time to analyze the situation and applied the DMAIC process, even if I did not complete the "meeting" portion.

Another coworker of mine had difficulty making decisions. If I brought a situation to Stu's attention, he would stew on it endlessly. I am not sure if he just couldn't make up his mind or was hoping some better choice would come along.

Applying the DMAIC process, I realized that Stu was not going to step up to decision making no matter how hard I tried. I found the best method for handling Stu was to tell, not ask. Again the process helped me define the approach, and I realized that I didn't need the meeting; I needed another way to handle him. I decided from then on that I would inform Stu what I was doing and why. By taking the decision-making responsibility away from him, more got done. I also found that by giving Stu a deadline for a decision (if I couldn't get around his approval by the first technique), it forced him to take a position. The important thing here was to identify a reason for the drop-dead date that made business sense and did not seem made up.

Another difficult coworker was a chronic complainer I will call "Winnie the Whiner." Winnie considered anything anyone asked her to do as unfair since she was already overwhelmed! Applying CPR, I realized I had to confront Winnie because she repeatedly was affecting both the business and the team's overall morale by complaining about every task, even the ones she did flawlessly. Using DMAIC, I recognized that the gap was not the work, but the method she used to say no. Frankly, this was a revelation. After analyzing the situation, I met with Winnie as a mentor, not a manager, and discussed how to say no (The *Try it Now* in Chapter 2). We also talked about prioritization and overall perception. Winnie stopped whining and has been promoted several times since.

You may also find that people whine and complain because they are overwhelmed, and it has nothing to do with their ability to say no. This often comes out when you meet with them, and something outside of work is usually at the heart of the problem.

Little Caesars can be especially scary to new hires and more reticent females. They love to rile everyone for the fun of it (at least they think it is fun). For some reason, perhaps a power trip, they just love to make a big deal out of an issue. One such coworker, Henry, was a manufacturing manager who just loved to get on his soapbox and complain about engineers. To some degree, Henry was flexing his muscles to make the manufacturing people feel that someone was in his corner. I also believe he thought confrontation was healthy, and perhaps it was. However, he made the more timid engineers afraid to make improvements. Applying CPR, I realized I had to confront Henry because his repeated comments were making the engineers less effective. I applied DMAIC and realized, in every case, Henry did have the best interest of the business at heart. As such, it was his ego that needed feeding. I found the best way to handle Henry was to ask him to be an integral part of the team looking to make the changes. At our meeting, we talked about ways to encourage the new engineers to think about manufacturing issues. By involving Henry in the technical problems early on, it satisfied his ego and also made sure the engineers were thinking about ease of manufacturing as they tried to implement some new process or product. Henry won, my team won, and IBM won.

Using CPR to decide if you should confront, and DMAIC as a structured approach to solving the problem, will help enormously in dealing with chronically difficult people and repeat offenders. The process takes time and practice, but the more you use it, the easier it gets. The main benefit is the process, so even if a situation does not exactly fit the DMAIC approach, using it can help you think objectively. I have found it especially helpful to those who have difficulty deciding whether the problem is them or the other person (something women tend to obsess about).

Unfortunately, you will find that sometimes situations occur where you need to respond immediately and do not have the luxury of taking such a carefully scientific approach. So what do you do? How you react can make all the difference. And your reaction should be based on the type of behavior these folks assume. By having some ready responses in your arsenal, you can often defuse these situations quickly.

For acute situations, just as with chronic situations, the very first step is to control yourself. In fact, it is even more important here. If you respond to the situation with anger, emotion, anxiety, or fear, you will be throwing fuel on the fire. If you find your voice getting louder, your heart beating faster, or your speech getting quicker, these are immediate warning signs that the person has your emotions under his or her control. Step back, count to three (ten is too long) and take a deep breath.

Having an arsenal of responses to use will build your confidence and help you keep your cool. Since the response depends on the individual types, you need to be able to identify them. The chart below indicates some of the difficult types I have experienced and how to spot them.

Renee's Rules
for Recognizing Difficult Types

Type	*Identifying Behavior*
Steamroller	Do it my way or else (also often a male chauvinist pig)
Monopolizer	Takes over and keeps everyone else from talking
Sniper	Snide remarks, trivializes comments
Minimizer	Tries to make you feel small
Grenade dropper	Unlike sniper, waits for one big surprise to drop
No person	Argues nothing will work but has no solution
Yes person	Agrees with everything, volunteers for everything, accomplishes little
Mr. or Ms. Invisible	Gives no feedback. If asked, says, "It doesn't matter."

Now let's discuss some "ready responses" with which you can arm yourself. I have found that they apply in almost every situation, with a little twist here and there on the words.

Let's begin with the steamroller. When a steamroller does not agree with what the group is proposing, he/she can become increasingly pushy, demanding, and disruptive. The steamroller is confrontational, wants everyone to do it his or her way, and is very hierarchical. (Much like an egotist—egotists become steamrollers when acute situations arise.) They are so strong-willed that they are not going to respond well if you are meek, but you also don't want to raise their boiling point.

Surprisingly, I have found the best response is very similar to how I treated my children when they misbehaved. With my toddlers, I addressed the problem firmly, assertively, and politely. If that didn't work, I suggested a time-out. With an adult this might sound like, "Let's slow down here. I understand you have a strong opinion about this but there are other opinions we would all like to hear as well." If the situation is too explosive, I might suggest, "Obviously we are not getting anywhere with this. Perhaps we should take a little break and re-address this later." If you cower, they continue. If you fight back, it feeds their anger. But if you just stand firm, they will normally realize it's time to take a break. (At that point, I might try to schedule some time later with the person where I can take time to apply the DMAIC principles.)

Monopolizing individuals (male and female) love to take over any conversation, meeting, or forum they can, even if they don't steamroll. When someone like this goes into expounding mode, I break in gently with, "Thanks, that's very helpful, but perhaps it's time to hear from someone else. Let's hear what _____ who has been waiting to speak has to offer." Or, "In the interest of keeping this meeting on time and giving everyone a chance to be heard, let's all try to keep our comments brief."

Snipers go on the attack by making remarks when you or others are speaking, since they love to look good by making fun of others. When you look at snipers and they don't agree, they will often roll their eyes. I find the most effective defense here is to attack back. Talk directly to him or her! Confront politely but firmly, saying something like, "I would appreciate if you would let me finish my point, and then I would be glad to hear what you have to say." If that doesn't work, I might use a stronger comment like, "Please, you are preventing the team from getting its work done. I would really appreciate if you could hold your comments until I am through." Be polite but assertive.

A related character is the minimizer. Minimizers don't snipe, but they will look for the right time to make what you are saying sound trivial. Above all, the best way to handle minimizers is to outsmart them (which frankly is rarely hard—after all, you usually know more about the topics being discussed than they do). Use facts, humor, and knowledge to stay on the point. Challenge his or her comments by asking, "Do you have any data to substantiate that?" When the minimizer answers that he/she has nothing specific, answer, "Well, I do have data, so let's review it." Minimizers look for a victim to make them feel more important. Eleanor Roosevelt once said, "no one can make you feel inferior without your consent." Don't give a minimizer your consent.

The grenade droppers are the last of the characters that typically use their ego to disarm you. They will save all their disagreements for one big "grenade" that they drop when they think you are on your weakest point. Here you truly need to remember to step back, take that deep breath, and stay in control. Again, I often use data here. When the grenade dropper throws his or her grenade, ask him or her to explain and enumerate each point. I have even written them down to allow him or her to feel you are giving them adequate attention. I then take each point and explain why it is incorrect. I have even put a line through the incorrect points as I discount them, defusing the grenade.

Of course, all of these actions are effective because you know what you are talking about, are prepared, and have the talent and expertise to back up your points. So my very best advice is to know your material and consider in advance where people might attack the data or recommendations.

One of my mentees went through one such situation. She had completed an analysis and made a minor math mistake. Another engineer with whom she did not get along well promptly sent an e-mail to a large number of people, including senior managers, pointing out her error. Since the error was small and had absolutely no impact on the final conclusion, she was extremely upset. I advised her to quickly correct the issue by sending an e-mail to every single person the engineer had copied. First, she should thank the individual for catching the issue; then, she should explain that she had recalculated with the recommended correction, and got the same end result. I encouraged her to explain very clearly why that factor had no impact on the result. By stating the facts, being armed with data, and showing that she knew her stuff, it was clear that the engineer had made a big deal over nothing, without actually saying it.

A *no* person can be a morale destroyer when you are trying to encourage a team toward a particular objective. This individual will often state that it will never work, frequently citing some prior time it was tried. My advice for the *no* people is to ask them directly, "Why did such a good idea fail? Was it in the execution? Was there something we might do differently this time to make it work better? We all believe in the result we want, and this idea should help achieve it, so how would you make sure it gets implemented more appropriately this time?"

On the other side of the coin, the *yes* person agrees with everything you propose and often volunteers to do any action you need. The problem is that you are not getting good feedback to enhance your ideas. Even worse, if you allow the *yes* people to take on the task, most likely they have signed up for so many other projects, yours may take a very distant backseat. With the *yes* person I respond, "Thanks for volunteering, but let's divide up the tasks at the end of the meeting to be sure we have everything covered."

I call the type of person who gives absolutely no feedback, verbal or otherwise, invisible. If you ask invisible people for an opinion, they respond, "It doesn't matter." Rather than accept that noncommittal answer, persist with, "Yes, it does, and your opinion matters to me. Do you agree with what we are suggesting or not?" After a while, invisible people will realize you are not going to ignore them or let them off the hook, and in most cases, they will start contributing to the meetings.

DMAIC as a process has been very helpful to me but again, it is only a process. In 99 percent plus of the cases where I applied it, it worked. But every once in a while there may be an employee you can't turn around, a coworker who is upset over something you have no ability to change, or someone who has gotten away with a behavior for so long he/she can't change it. If you have tried the process, consulted HR or management for advice, and gone through all the steps without success, then you should not feel like a failure. If you had to fire people for performance, the fault was theirs, not yours.

While this chapter is about difficult people, I do want to acknowledge that throughout my career I had many excellent managers and coworkers. The ones I mentioned above were certainly an exception to the rule. Moreover, it was the exception that I had to step in with such drastic countermeasures. However, even some of my favorite managers sometimes had their moments (as did I).

One excellent manager, to whom I could speak frankly in any career or business discussion and who facilitated many opportunities for me, was an easily excitable type. I mean that in a positive way because his excitement brought out the best in people. However, when he got excited, he would often raise his voice (this could happen when he was upset or delighted). When he'd get loud, it was my normal human reaction to answer back loudly. Amazingly, I found this always worked negatively. He'd turn to me and say, "Now, don't get emotional." Or at other times, I'd see him actually tune me out. I learned from this that a much more effective method for getting people to listen to a woman was to be totally unemotional, factual, and speak clearly and softly. So when he got loud, I became more soft-spoken, and he listened to everything I said.

In general, this is excellent advice for women. Men apparently can somehow tolerate emotion in other men, but they are less comfortable with it in women. If you are hurt, upset, angry, excited, whatever, don't show it. The most effective way to have others really listen is to speak softly yet affirmatively with confidence. Margaret Thatcher once advised, "Speak at the same volume as your opponent until he stops interrupting." This may work in a political debate, but I have found that with certain individuals and situations it can backfire. I prefer to start with the calm, soft-spoken approach to bring everyone back down to a civil level. But if it doesn't work, then don't be afraid to crank up the decibels. Just don't stay there. When you regain control, bring the sound level back down.

This behavior works with children also. When I was a teacher, it was common for me to get laryngitis each winter. The days in which I taught with almost no voice and had to speak very slowly but quietly were the days where the class was absolutely on its best behavior. They had to stay very quiet and attentive to hear what I was teaching, and you could hear a pin drop in the room. Try to catch yourself when you start to get emotional or loud. You may feel very justified in your emotion, but the effect will be the exact opposite of what you hope to achieve.

Cultural norms and behaviors can affect how individuals speak. For example, Asian American women tend to speak softly; Hispanic women tend to speak more loudly. Here, changing your decibel level can be even more effective as when you speak out of your normal character you get attention.

A section on difficult people for women would not be complete without at least mentioning sexual harassment. In the workplace, this can take several forms, from inappropriate comments to more blatant actions. My advice here is you do *not* have to take it. It is against the law. If someone makes you uncomfortable with an action, tell him or her and also inform your management. I once had a supplier make inappropriate advances during a business trip, and I told him I was happily married and had no interest in pursuing anything else. I never informed anyone, but he never repeated anything inappropriate, and we were able to work together after that. Had he repeated anything less than totally business appropriate behavior, I would have reported it. There is a fine line between acceptable dating of someone who may work in your company and seeing someone who can have an impact on your career. IBM typically tries to keep married or dating individuals in separate organizations where one employee cannot impact the success or failure of the other. (Although the company doesn't always know who is dating whom.) It would be completely inappropriate for a manager to have his or her significant other in his or her organization.

Harassment can take other forms than purely sexual. Inappropriate behavior should never be ignored, and the longer it goes on, the more the individual thinks it is okay. Sometimes you may not be sure, and in those cases seek advice. I know of an individual in another firm whose male manager made some suggestive remarks to her. She wasn't sure whether he was being funny or suggestive. My advice to her was to make sure someone else knew about what occurred, document it, and also let the individual know she found the remarks uncomfortable. The behavior never recurred, but if it had, she could establish that she had tried to stop it, and this was repeat behavior. Once again, harassment is illegal, and you don't need to take it. If your management is involved, go to your HR advisor, legal department, or someone else you can trust in your firm. If you are in a small company where you don't have these avenues, seek outside counsel.

Blatant harassment is much less common than little suggestive comments. I had a friend who was told by a manager she wore her blouses buttoned up too high. Another acquaintance of mine was told she couldn't get promoted because she was living with someone, and they weren't married. In both of these cases, the issues occurred years before, and the individuals ignored the comments. However, they were bothered by them for the rest of their careers, and in my mind, they should have responded more definitively when they occurred.

I do need to note that everything I have been recommending in this chapter has been focused on dealing with coworkers, bosses, and employees to make your business run more effectively. However, when you are dealing with a customer, *do not* apply these techniques directly. There is an old saying, "The customer is always right, even when he/she is wrong." And I completely subscribe to this principle. In these cases, you want to bend over backward to keep the customer happy to the degree you can. The DMAIC process can help you define the situation, but your response has to be tailored to meet the customer's need. In many cases, the key is giving the individuals time to vent and to feel that their concerns are being heard. People working at help desks are trained in listening and empathizing, which provides a catharsis for many people to work off their anger. I have a friend who is a nursing instructor who teaches that a nurse's number one job is to listen to the patient and the patient's family. Since this book is directed toward women in industry, I am not focusing on situations like this, but don't make the mistake of confronting a customer or taking their anger personally. It is almost never directed at you but is about their situation or concern. Better to hand the customer off to a supervisor or someone specifically experienced in their issues than to get into any type of confrontation.

Finally, try to recognize when the stress, situation, or difficult individual is causing you to move outside your reasonableness zone and *you* become the difficult person. If you find yourself raising your voice, if your pulse is beating faster, if you are clenching your fists, or if you feel like crying, it is time to cool off before you say or do something you will regret. Breathe deeply, excuse yourself, take a walk, kick the wall, call someone you can unload on, or practice whatever technique releases your tension; but get it back under control.

Everyone has the right to their opinions and emotions, but if you experience these warning signals, listen to them and find a way to recenter. My son-in-law who teaches meditation reminds me often that "the conditions don't create your mood, your mood creates the conditions."

Unless you live and work in Utopia, you will encounter difficult individuals in your career. Handling them, confronting situations when they occur, and recognizing the warning signs in yourself are not easy skills. They take practice, and you may have some setbacks along the way. Attack the problem, not the person. You will feel better, and your work environment will be less stressful. The difference between winning and losing is how everyone pulls together. One rotten apple can spoil a bunch, so attack the issue promptly and effectively.

8

DARE I ASK?
NEGOTIATING FOR YOURSELF

If you don't know where you're going, you'll
wind up somewhere else.

—*Yogi Berra*

This is probably the most important chapter in this book for advancing your career. If you read nothing else, read this chapter!

As a director, technical leader, and senior manager in IBM, I have mentored many new and experienced female and male engineers throughout my career. Invariably, I found differences between the sexes when I held these mentoring sessions. Following are some pitfalls that women seem to fall into much more often than men.

One of the questions I ask mentees in their first mentoring session is where they want to be in five years. In almost every case, the male mentees could identify either the job or the type of job they wanted next, typically a very specific answer. The females, on the other hand, almost always answered that they wanted to be in a job where they could contribute to the business and be appreciated. While this is a noble concept, frankly, it is a vague answer. What's worse, those few women who could state their goals typically had less lofty ones than their male counterparts. The males typically saw themselves one or two levels higher than the females.

This behavior is a major factor in why women have trouble breaking the glass ceiling. Women are doing it to themselves! Successful people have goals, they know when to expect to reach them, and they let their management team know what they are. I have found that most women wait passively to be tapped on the shoulder while most men are actively seeking their next goal. I have fallen into this trap myself, and it is something I still have to work at regularly. The first step is recognizing it.

Career success is defining what you want and achieving it. As such, how can a woman reach the same success as a man if she hasn't decided what it is she wants? So let's spend some time on goal setting. First of all, what are goals? I have heard a goal defined as "an ambition with a schedule." For me, it is being able to answer the following questions: Where do you want to be in the next six months? Two years? Five years? Goals need to be specific and measurable.

Women are excellent at setting technical or business goals. They can clearly state the steps involved, the dates when each step will be achieved, and the way to measure their success. But in my observations, when the goal becomes personal or career related, women become clueless. Most self-help books talk about smart goals (specific, measureable, applied, realistic, and timed), so I will not belabor this. However, the questions below will help you get started.

Try It Now
Do You Have Smart Goals?

- Can you write down the goal? This is something I make every mentee do in our second coaching session. With some females, it is like pulling teeth.
- Do you have a specific job in mind? Can you name someone doing it today? If this is a new position, can you describe it in detail? This is usually easier for female mentees to answer than number one.
- How long will it take to get to that goal?
- How will you know you are on track?
- What dependencies do you have (you, your manager, education, other people, project completion, family, whatever), and what are you doing to assure they are in place?

Once you have the answers to these five questions, you will have crossed a critical hurdle in moving up in your career, but it's only the first step. As I stated earlier, even after I mentor and advise the males and females to define their goals, I find the females invariably don't reach as high. This became very clear to me some years ago when two comparable new hires, male and female, came to me for mentoring at almost the same time in their careers. The female actually had better grades and a stronger college record, yet the male saw himself moving faster in his career than the female! He also had a more aggressive goal. I have found this behavior, time and again, when mentoring. If success is meeting your goal and a male has stretched himself more, then the odds are he will more than likely get further. If the male falls short of his goal and the woman gets to hers, the male will still have moved forward faster! I cannot emphasize this enough. Women don't expect enough of themselves!

Another inconsistency I find is that women are excellent at looking at new and innovative ways to push a task beyond the status quo. They are relentless negotiators when they are asking for a piece of capital equipment, support for a business or technical need, or support for team recognition. Yet when asked to apply these same talents to their career, they again become clueless. The talent and ability is in there someplace, but I find that the confidence and belief that they deserve this is lacking. So I have added a final step to the goal setting process.

Try It Now
The Difference between Smart Goals and Having SMARTS!

- Benchmark yourself against a comparable male or fast-tracker on the *speed* of your promotions and opportunities. This will help you do a career "reality check" on whether you are *stretching yourself* enough. These are what give you **SMARTS**.

- Another way to answer question 6 is to consider the three Bs:
    1. Are your goals *big?*
    2. Are your goals *brave?*
    3. Are your goals *beyond your comfort zone?*

In smaller companies without clear equal opportunity policies, you should be especially vigilant. A young female attorney with five years of practice asked my advice when she learned that a new male associate she was training had negotiated a starting salary greater than hers. I asked her if she had even negotiated her starting salary, and she looked at me with horror. After a lengthy discussion, she agreed she needed to approach her boss with a request for equity. I asked her what that meant, and she indicated she wanted to have her salary raised to that of her trainee! (I told you women don't ask for enough.) She was an excellent attorney and had brought much business into the firm. I reminded her that she should ask for more as she had also brought experience and new clients to the firm. I told her to prepare her case just as she would prepare a case for a judge. She did so and was immediately given an appropriate increase. By the way, she recently became the youngest partner in her firm. She clearly had taken this advice to heart. (She was also an excellent attorney—remember, results matter.)

I attended an IBM-sponsored negotiating workshop taught by Linda Babcock from Carnegie Mellon that crystallized many of my observations into actual studies. She described that in her university, female undergraduates were complaining that the males were being given teaching assignments while the females were simply teaching assistants. When they investigated why this supposedly unfair treatment was condoned, it turned out that there was only one reason, the men asked! The men felt they could handle teaching on their own and asked for the opportunity. The women were waiting for someone to tell them they were ready and never asked. The implications of this are huge. By teaching in college versus being a teaching assistant, the males had a better resume and could ask for more money when they applied for a job! By starting out making more, they continued to get increases over this starting salary and ended up better paid.

I have found similar behavior as I interviewed and hired new engineers into IBM. The males typically challenged the initial offer much more often than the females. It's almost as though the males saw this as a sports competition and approached it with relish. The woman received the offer and assumed that was it. Now IBM has a clear policy of equal opportunity and new-hire salaries are carefully watched for equity, but when someone pushes a little harder for a larger sign-on bonus, or for more moving and living, a truly worthy candidate often gets it. The women just don't typically think to ask for this. In her studies, Babcock found that 7 percent of women negotiate their salary when hired, while amazingly 57 percent of men do! Moreover, a 2007 study by *Catalyst Magazine* showed that even when women do negotiate, they are satisfied with less! When you consider that further increases are typically a percentage of that starting salary, this can be a huge impact to lifetime earnings.

So what advice can I give women to fix this inequity? For me, a great supporter was my husband. Having a competitive male frequently reminding me of my worth and encouraging me to ask was a tremendous help. Is there an aggressive male figure to whom you can go for advice? Find a friend, a mentor, a coach, someone who understands you and your capabilities. Use that person as a sounding board. Or, if you know a successful woman who has overcome this "disability," go to her. Go over those goals with this person and ask, "Am I challenging myself enough? Do you think I could go faster or higher?" Most situations have more room for negotiation than you think! A mentor once told me, "If people never say no to you, you aren't asking for enough!" My experience has been that men ask for more than they deserve and often get it, while women don't ask even when they deserve it.

Remember, if you ask and they say no, you are at the very same place as if you never asked! Remember also that asking can never be emotional. A pleasant, factual, unemotional, and well-practiced approach is essential. My earlier rules for making sure people listen apply here as well as some basic questions to ask yourself.

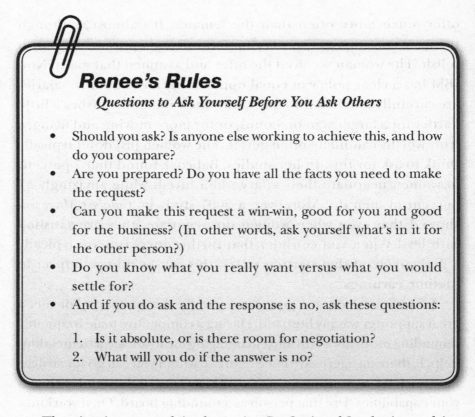

Renee's Rules

Questions to Ask Yourself Before You Ask Others

- Should you ask? Is anyone else working to achieve this, and how do you compare?
- Are you prepared? Do you have all the facts you need to make the request?
- Can you make this request a win-win, good for you and good for the business? (In other words, ask yourself what's in it for the other person?)
- Do you know what you really want versus what you would settle for?
- And if you do ask and the response is no, ask these questions:

  1. Is it absolute, or is there room for negotiation?
  2. What will you do if the answer is no?

The win-win approach is a key point. Professional fund-raisers advise that people are generous because they get something out of their gift, so learn what they value. By knowing what will help the person you are negotiating with achieve what they need, you can direct your request to satisfy it.

I am not implying that you should go out there and demand everything from your management. What I am recommending is not to be satisfied with the status quo or just the normal rate and pace of career growth. If you are good at what you do, apply some of that talent to career management as well. And if you do get into a negotiation, career discussion, interview, or other opportunity, spend some time asking if you have pushed yourself enough and also what will happen if they say no. Know the minimum you would accept. Is there some appropriate compromise that you are willing to accept? Role-play the meeting and practice your points. This will go a long way toward overcoming your anxiety.

This is what I did when asking for my first salary increase. Remember, I had been rehired by IBM after leaving ten years earlier and teaching part-time during that period. When I was rehired, I was brought back at the same level at which I had left the company ten years earlier, despite having university experience and maturity. I never thought to ask for more, and since the salary was considerably better than I could make teaching, I returned to industry.

After my first six months, it was clear I was having a very positive impact on the business and technical results of our area, and I was being given more and more difficult leadership assignments. My immediate manager had changed. (I had four managers in my first year.) My husband, my aggressive male cheerleader, was constantly telling me I was underpaid for what I was doing and kept encouraging me to ask for an increase. Finally, I got up my nerve and asked for a meeting with my manager, who was really depending on me for a lot of items. (This was number three of the four managers I had that first year.)

He started the meeting by telling me he was very pleased with my contributions and wanted to know how I felt I was doing. I told him I thought I was having a very positive impact and that I had only one concern. He asked me what that was, and I responded, "I really think I am underpaid for the responsibility I am taking on." I explained how I had been brought back at the same level that I had been at ten years before and that I really felt I was performing at a higher level. The new manager, who had only been in the job a few weeks, pulled out my personnel records, and when he looked at the paperwork, his eyes became huge. It was clear he had not yet looked at what I was making and was quite amazed at how low my salary was. He answered that he would look into it. One week later, I had an increase! Three months later, I had an out-of-plan promotion (he argued I had been brought back at too low a level and was fixing that), and one year later I was promoted again (in plan this time)—and under a new (the fourth) manager.

There are several lessons to learn here: (1) Don't assume your manager knows what you make, especially if there have been many organization changes. (2) It helps to have an understanding of the pay scale and what others at similar performance and responsibility are getting. However, don't compare yourself to an individual.

Managers will avoid those types of discussions at best and, at worst, get defensive. (3) If I hadn't asked, I am sure I would not have seen three increases in one year, and all I asked about was the first one. (4) You need to negotiate from a position of strength. Asking for a raise when you haven't been doing the job or have been taking a lot of time off or have not delivered on your commitments is not appropriate. (Remember—results matter.) In this negotiation, it's important to have confidence in your worth and to have a list of key accomplishments and their impact prepared. You may never need to refer to them, but just preparing that list will bolster your confidence. In addition, your manager may have forgotten some or may not even realize them all. Again, I am not recommending you spend a lot of time on the specifics, but if you are asked questions or need examples, having made that list is very helpful. If others (customers, coworkers) have complimented you, sent notes about your performance, or asked for you on a given project, it's good to have those examples in your back pocket as well.

Timing is also important. If your company gives annual raises, don't wait until after evaluations and raises are completed to have the conversation. Then, it's more like sour grapes. When you've just completed a really significant project that delighted everyone and are ready to start a new assignment, it's a perfect time to initiate the discussion about your salary and future opportunities.

When management asks you to take on a new job or assignment, it is a totally appropriate time to ask about what is in it for you. The very best increases and promotions I received were when I was asked to fix something that was not running well, and they wanted me for the job. Instead of jumping to say yes (that very female behavior), I learned to ask, "Okay, I am certainly glad to do whatever it takes to help the business, but what is in it for me personally? Why is it better than continuing on the path I am currently on?" In almost every case, management sweetened the pot on the offer. Again, it was not a threat or a refusal but an objective question asking for an assessment of why I should consider that position versus the one I had.

A few final points for your salary discussions: Always focus on the business and the job. It is totally inappropriate to expect your manager to give you an increase because you are living above your means or have a lot of unexpected bills. Keep your personal financial situation out of this discussion. Knowing your manager and making sure he/she is aware of your accomplishments (this could even be periodic quick e-mails) over the long haul makes this meeting even more positive. Also, you should never threaten, as that will put your manager on the defensive, or worse, you might have to follow through on your threat when you didn't really mean it in the first place.

I am not recommending pushing your management team into something unreasonable. What I am recommending is that you push, prepare, and promote yourself, just as I pushed my young attorney friend.

Speaking of promotions, men also do a better job of preparing for their next promotion. They put out feelers earlier, both with their peers and within their management chain. They ask early on what is required to reach the promotion and then let others know they are seeking it. In many technical, business, and management fields, certain positions require demonstration of your worth. For example, many companies have positions like senior technical staff member or certified project manager that require certification, patents, publications, or key leadership assignments. I was the executive sponsor for an IBM Women in Technology networking group, and in one of our meetings I described the requirements for various promotional levels within our company. Many of the women were surprised that they could even get this information, let alone have asked for it. When I provided them with out a set of blank and sample forms that they could use to assess their own readiness for promotion, they were even more astonished. Men are also good at asking many questions about new job opportunities or promotions. They ask about whether the area is growing, what new opportunities for advancement it will provide, when they should expect to see a financial impact, etc. Women focus on the next assignment as an end in itself rather than a path to something else.

Try It Now
Prepare Your Promotion Package

A good exercise to work on is to prepare the justification for your next promotion. If you are targeting a specific position, like a partnership, high-level technical assignment, program management, or some other business level, your company most likely has a set of forms you need to complete to create this justification. In other firms, it may be less regimented, but you still need to demonstrate your competence and readiness for your next position.

Write your promotion "package" using the appropriate format your company uses for this position. If no standard form exists, pull together your own qualifications and create your own package.

When you have completed it, share it with your manager and your mentor, specifically to identify your weakest areas and how to improve them.

As you read this, you may feel I am generalizing and that the many women in high levels in many companies have already overcome these issues. Wrong! I recently attended a panel discussion by women executives from several companies, large and small. During the panel, a member of the audience asked, "If you knew then what you know now, what would you have done differently?" In almost every case, these highly paid, very successful women said, "I would have asked for more."

One of these individuals, who is at the top echelon of a major *Fortune 500* company, described an experience she had with her daughter. The daughter had just been offered a position with a new firm that was exactly the type of work she wanted. She asked her mother for some advice about the interview and the offer. Her mother, a high-powered executive, thought it was a great start. However, they had the foresight to bring in a career coach who advised the daughter to ask for more money and helped her frame her arguments as to why that was appropriate. As a result, her daughter got a considerably larger starting salary. The high-powered female executive admitted, "I was so delighted with her opportunity, I never thought to have her ask for more."

Another weakness women seem to have that impacts their overall negotiating strength is their dislike of bragging. I am always amazed when my husband accomplishes something that I consider "his job," and he reminds his management how it would not have happened without his involvement. He does it in a factual way and makes sure his contribution is known. I see this with the men I work with, the men who work for me, and the men I work for. They are very comfortable tooting their own horns. So why can't women? (Remember the exercise in Chapter 2? This would be an excellent time to revisit it.) I have seen many women hesitate to bring a good project or idea forward because it "wasn't finished yet" or "it wasn't perfect." A man would often bring an equivalent forward, indicating it needed some work but bragging about its potential. Men maximize their achievements; women minimize theirs.

It is human nature to respond to people who ask you for more by giving them more. One of my friends likes to tell the story of her twin daughters. One was the type to accept what her parents told her and rarely pushed them into changing their position. The other was the opposite—she would argue her case, with such cogent facts that they often relented. As such, one twin would lament they were being easier on her sister. Their answer was, she never pushed back. Once the "easier" twin realized this, she also started pushing the status quo. (Much to the chagrin of my friend and her husband; but truly, something that made the second twin a stronger person.)

Like it or not, the world is not fair. People do move ahead based on results and accomplishments, but the rate depends on what challenges you set for yourself. You keep your technical skills honed. So why not do the same with your negotiating skills? If you feel these are lacking, take a class in negotiation. Practice.

Now that we have established that women are less prone to ask, how can you make sure you are managing your opportunities? Start by keeping your managers aware of your interests. Ask for a meeting with a higher level of management. In IBM we called these skip levels. Other companies may refer to them as executive interviews. Regardless of the name, it is an opportunity for senior management to meet you. Let them know your aspirations and ask for their help to achieve them.

Another difference I have found between men and women is in sharing career opportunities. Men are very open about mentioning the jobs to which they are applying and even welcome other men to apply for the same opportunity. Women do the opposite. Rarely will they mention a new assignment they are pursuing to their coworkers, perhaps because they don't want anyone to know if they don't get it or because they don't want competition. This is not because they think the other person may take the position away from them, but more that the women are worried about jeopardizing their friendship or working relationship if they get the job. If you are looking for other opportunities that may be out there, you will learn more by asking the men rather than the women.

When it comes to pushing themselves, there is another force that can hold women back financially. They are less likely to put money first when making career decisions because they want work-life flexibility, personal fulfillment, or less risk.

One other point when you are changing areas. Consider the timing to be sure you are not losing out on something. For example, in some companies your year-end bonus is given based on the area you are working in on some specific date. If you leave or change areas before this date, you may be foregoing this bonus. I have a friend who moved into a different division in her company in November. This division had a lower performance against the company's objectives and therefore gave lower bonuses. Since she was a member of that new division on December 31, she ended up losing the difference in bonus between the divisions. Had she transferred January 1, she would not have lost that. I do believe a man would have made it a ground rule that he not lose the bonus monies before accepting the change. This never occurred to the female, nor had it ever occurred to me.

Another example of activities that can happen behind the scenes occurred with a friend of mine. She had interviewed for another position within her company and was among the top candidates. Her manager had approved her interviewing, and she was very interested in the assignment. However, she was not offered the position because the offering manager consulted with a senior manager in her management chain who indicated that she was critical to the current area and with a new business opportunity occurring there, he thought the firm would be better served by not moving her. Luckily, the offering manager was very open with the individual and let her know about these conversations. When this friend told me about her situation, I advised her to speak to her management chain in a righteously indignant but pleasant manner and ask what gives. If she was so valuable, what were they doing to keep her happy? This led to some options and additional financial incentives for the individual. So keep your ear to the ground. Interviewing for other positions can lead to opportunities even if you don't change assignments.

In Lewis Carrol's *Alice in Wonderland*, Alice asked the Cheshire cat which path she should take. The Cheshire cat responded, "Where do you want to go?" Alice replied that she didn't care. So the cat logically concluded, "Then it doesn't matter which way you go." I can think of nothing worse in your career than spending thirty years with no goal and no purpose. It does matter which way you go. However, taking a side path because it fills a need for you professionally, personally, or spiritually should never be discounted. Just understand why you are doing it. I left IBM to be home with my children until they started school. It was a conscious decision, and I am glad I did it. So reprioritize your goals when it's time to take a side trip. But when you return to the main road, be sure you are traveling at a speed right for you.

9

IT'S WHO YOU KNOW

Every person on earth is no more than
six "degrees of separation" from everyone else.
—*Frigyes Karinthy, Hungarian author*

Imagine that you just received an invitation to a networking event. You don't know anyone who is attending, but the group will include executives, senior managers, and top professionals from both within and outside your firm. What do you do?

Do you dread it? Maybe you go out and buy a new outfit. Perhaps you tell yourself you don't really need to go because you are already on a good path in your company or because you want to "make it" on your own. Do you dust off your business cards and make sure the information is correct?

If any of these reactions sound familiar, this chapter is for you. It provides a refresher course in networking with exercises to turn you into a pro.

I used to be one of those people who cringed at the thought of networking. After all, I was a scientist, and my favorite place to be was in the laboratory. However, I realized that I had to learn to network or no one would ever know what I was accomplishing in that laboratory. I read some books, watched others who seemed to network naturally, developed some basic skills, and learned how to prepare for these events. Now, I look forward to them, and you can, too—by practicing the exercises in this chapter. Much of what you will learn is common sense, yet it has the potential to change your life!

An extremely important point for women is that there are many ways men network that don't naturally include women. So women need to be even more aware of how to maximize their networking opportunities.

114

Why do you need to network? There is an old riddle, "If a tree falls in a forest and no one hears it, did it make a sound?" My variation on this is, "If you do an excellent job and no one knows you did it, did you really do a good job?" Of course ability matters, but exposure is every bit as important. Being "in the right place at the right time" is not just who you know but who knows the people you know.

Networking can happen when you least expect it. My husband, John, a lifelong resident of our community, was always interested in new construction and developments in our town. One evening we attended, of all things, a wake for the grandfather of our daughter's friend. While waiting in the line to enter the funeral home, we ran into my coworker, Marv. I introduced him to John and as we exchanged how we were connected to the deceased, Marv mentioned that he was the chairperson of our town planning board. John told Marv that he had always wanted to do something like that and if he ever had an opening to keep him in mind. Marv answered, "Well, it just so happens we have an opening coming up, but you need to be sponsored by your town councilperson. He's over there. Let me introduce you." A month later, John was sworn in as a member of the planning board and some years later succeeded Marv as chairperson. He has also taken on numerous other public service tasks that have given him a lot of satisfaction *and* brought him new connections for his business.

My second example is Bill Gates. Everyone knows that Microsoft got its beginning by being chosen to provide the operation system, DOS, for IBM's first personal computer. What most people don't know is that several companies were being considered for this role and at the time Microsoft was a startup without a lot of proven performance. However, Bill Gates's mother, Mary Maxwell Gates, happened to be on the executive board of the United Way. Sitting with her on the board was John Akers, CEO of IBM. Mary made Akers aware of her son's business, Akers informed Don Estridge, who was leading the task force to bring the PC out in record time, and the rest is history.

In my own career in IBM, I realized that knowing the right people was a critical aspect of growing my opportunities. The more people who knew my talents and asked for my help, the more valued by management I became. The more problems I solved, the more people

I came to know who would ask me for advice. In every promotion, but especially as I reached distinguished engineer and director level, the promoting management team had to present evidence of my impact across the business, not just in our local area. It was the breadth and responsibilities of the people who knew me and could vouch for my abilities that made the difference.

When I left IBM and began my new career of coaching women in business and technology, my first steps were to expand my network in this arena. I had always been involved in the women in technology organizations, but I stepped up my interactions. I offered to teach a class at the Society of Women Engineers convention and started reconnecting to people I had met at other organizations. I contacted executives and personnel in many companies that I had worked with over the years and informed the Women in Technology groups within IBM of my new role. Each of these led to new contacts, and before I knew it, I was getting requests from several companies and was even offered a job (which I declined) with a career consulting firm.

The point of all these examples is that networking is an essential part of everyone's career. It happens when a person who wants something makes it known to someone else who can help or knows someone who can help.

How many people do you know? The average person knows about 250 people. If you consider that each of these 250 people knows 250 people who know 250 people, you have the potential to reach fifteen million people!

Networking is a chain reaction you cannot ignore. For example, most companies have internal job postings, and you may use them to look for a new position. But be aware that more than 90 percent of the jobs in these postings are actually filled by someone the hiring manager or one of his or her associates knows! Never underestimate the power of a friend of a friend (of a friend!).

Since networking with people can unleash a chain reaction, it is important to make sure that the chain is projecting you forward in a positive light. That happens when you strengthen your ties to people.

In their book *Make Your Contacts Count,* Baber and Waymon indicate that people you know can fall into one of six categories: accidents, acquaintances, associates, actors, advocates, and allies. The higher the connection, the more likely the individuals are to recommend you or your services. So how do you build these links? Since I am a scientist, I use the scientific definition: symbiosis.

Symbiosis in science is the process of one organism living off another such that both organisms thrive. In other words, giving and receiving. You only control one of these two acts, but the process of helping—or what one of my managers called "back-scratching"— usually pays back manyfold. It is the key way to strengthen your ties to people and make them notice you.

Try It Now

Your Connections

- List twenty people with whom you interact who are in a position to impact your career or personal goals. They can be peers, managers, employees, clients, friends, you name it.

- Now on a scale of 1 to 10—where 10 is the strongest connection (someone who will go to bat for you without being asked), 1 is the weakest (someone who might or might not remember your name), and 5 is average (someone you work with who is neutral about your abilities and potential)—rate each person.

- Where do the people on your list fall? If there are very few over the 5 mark, you need to do some symbiosis, especially with the individuals who can help you the most.

How can you start the symbiosis process? It begins with knowing who you are already helping.

Try It Now
Who Are You Helping?

- How do you know whether you are helping others? Keep a list! For the next week, keep a list of all the requests and favors you have done for any of the twenty influential people you just identified (and others if they come along during that week). Just keep track and don't analyze, yet.

- At the end of the week, consider your list.

  1. Have you interacted with any of the twenty in a positive way?
  2. Were you spending much more of your time doing items for people not on this list?
  3. Did you put any off because you were too busy?
  4. Did you meet the requestor's expectations?
  5. Did you go far beyond what was asked (which is very female but not necessarily a good thing)?
  6. Did you respond more quickly to requests from more senior managers or people who were in a position to help you the most?

The point of this exercise is not to turn you into a scorekeeper or someone who only does things for people who can help in return. However, by looking at the time you are spending over the course of a week interacting and helping others, you can get a clear picture of whether you are strengthening your relationships with others. If your list is short, you need to look for opportunities to help others—and they are everywhere.

Women tend to make a critical mistake when they practice symbiosis, and it often backfires. They do more than they are asked to do. If you overdo, two negatives can occur. First, people will expect it the next time. Even worse, people may be insulted that you felt they couldn't do it by themselves.

Symbiotic helping is not telling others what you would do in their shoes or what they *should* do. It is taking some task, problem, issue, or activity off someone's workload and onto yours so you both benefit. If you have helped others, you rarely need to remind them when you need their help.

If you had trouble identifying twenty names for this exercise, you definitely need to get to more networking events. Where do you find them? The answer to that question is another question: What do you want to achieve?

Try It Now

Why Are You Networking?

- Are you looking to meet new clients, potential employers, potential employees?
- Do you want to meet others (men and women) who have made it to the level you hope to achieve?
- Do you want to overcome a fear that is holding you back?
- Do you want to meet people with similar jobs in different firms?
- Do you want to change jobs?
- Are you looking for marketing opportunities?
- Or are your goals something else entirely?

Write down your top few goals.

The answers to this exercise will help you decide what types of networking you want to do. Then where do you go? Check out the professional societies that exist in your field. Go to company-sponsored training classes. Attend more business meetings whenever possible. Ask your mentors where they network and whether you can tag along.

Find out if your company has any networking or diversity groups. Join the Chamber of Commerce.

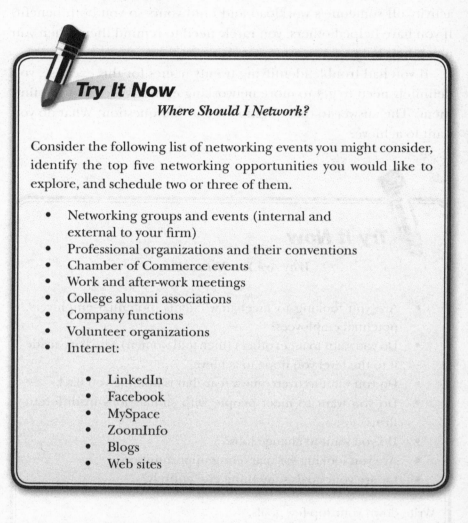

Try It Now
Where Should I Network?

Consider the following list of networking events you might consider, identify the top five networking opportunities you would like to explore, and schedule two or three of them.

- Networking groups and events (internal and external to your firm)
- Professional organizations and their conventions
- Chamber of Commerce events
- Work and after-work meetings
- College alumni associations
- Company functions
- Volunteer organizations
- Internet:

  - LinkedIn
  - Facebook
  - MySpace
  - ZoomInfo
  - Blogs
  - Web sites

Networking can happen anywhere, so be prepared. Marketing classes advise you to prepare an elevator speech when you are trying to convince a client quickly. The idea is, if you meet a client in an elevator, what could you say to make the right impression and allow a follow-up. My analogy is what would you say to your division president, CEO, or other bigwig if you met them in an elevator? While this may be somewhat unlikely to occur in a large organization, what often happens is that you are invited to a luncheon, recognition event, or some other company function where senior executives will be attending. When you sit down at the table and introduce yourself, how can you make that meeting memorable?

Try It Now
Prepare Your "Elevator" Speech

What would you say if you had the opportunity to meet your CEO, division president, or other senior executive at a meeting, dinner, or other company function?

1. Introduce yourself with simple definition of your responsibilities (see next exercise on "What Do You Do?").
2. In advance, read about the individual and his/her initiatives on your company's intranet and on the Internet. Prepare a question to ask about the progress in this area that demonstrates your knowledge of the initiatives.
3. Listen.

Since the elevator meeting is a chance occurrence, and company events with executives don't happen frequently, consider some less-traditional places to purposely connect. Men frequently look for opportunities to be seen by people they believe can enhance their careers. They will go to upper-level meetings even if it is not necessary they be there, and they look for opportunities to "run into" people who have more influence.

Here's an example from my IBM days. I found many women sat at their workstation over lunch rather than going to the cafeteria or local restaurant, since women are excellent at multitasking. Most of my male coworkers, especially those looking to "fast-track," made a point of going to the cafeteria during the time their managers or managers' managers ate. Naturally, they would sit down at their table and start a conversation. I ask you, who actually accomplished more over lunch? Even when the females did go to the cafeteria, which was infrequent, they sat with peers and coworkers.

Be on the alert for networking opportunities wherever you go. I have heard of great connections made by listening to someone in the line at the grocery store, at the gym, or on the train.

As a woman, there are some places the "old boy's network" haunts that may be difficult for you to break into. Many deals and connections happen on the golf course. Even excellent female golfers are not invited to play as often as less-skilled males. I had one executive in IBM advise me to learn golf as he had found it a wonderful source of connections, but I could never really compete there. Instead, I worked to identify other opportunities. For example, we organized a quarterly executive women's "dinner out" where we went to different restaurants, and everyone was encouraged to bring someone else along. This group still meets, and new folks attend every time. I also used the "cafeteria" connection whenever possible.

In today's digital world, there is a huge potential source of connections, the Internet. With opportunities like Facebook, My Space, email, blogs, chat rooms, and instant messaging, the number of ways to expand your Internet connections is exploding. These are generally weaker ties, but nevertheless the typical person who knows 250 people can easily quadruple this through the Internet. People may not know your face, but they know your name, and through them, you can connect to others. If your company has an intranet or internally sponsored networking site, use that as well. You never know when it will pay back, but it will.

One example of this occurred when I attended a conference 3000 miles from home. I did not know anyone in the room and sat down in an empty seat between two other individuals. I turned to the woman on my right and introduced myself. She exclaimed, "Renee Weisman, I just participated in a NetMeeting where you presented last week." I read her nametag and realized that I not only knew her name but wanted to get some support from her organization.

That might not seem so unusual except I then turned to introduce myself to the woman on my left. She exclaimed, "Renee Weisman, we IM'd just last week! Did you ever get the information you were looking for?"

Both of these connections, which were weakly established though the Internet, became much stronger at the conference. What's more, I did not feel alone anymore as we made plans to meet later at dinner.

So, let's get back to the basics. Once you have defined where you want to go to grow your network, your next step is to meet as many people as you can.

Take a deep breath and count slowly: One thousand one. One thousand two. One thousand three. You have just passed the amount of time it takes to make a first impression!

You only have one chance to make a first impression, so make it a good one. If you are a person who has trouble coming up with small talk or remembering the names of the people you just met, the exercises in this chapter can help.

As you meet people, they are most likely as uncomfortable as you. So smile, be welcoming, shake their hand firmly, and make eye contact. Look at their faces, not their hands. When a person says his or her name, be sure to get it right. Repeat it as you shake hands: "It's nice to meet you, Jennifer," or "Maxwell, that's my grandson's name." Just repeating the name makes sure you have it right *and* helps you remember it. If the person is wearing a name tag, make sure you get the pronunciation right. My name is Renee, and it is always mispronounced. So when someone takes the time to learn to say my name properly, I appreciate it and remember it. I also use this as a means of repeating my name to help others remember it. ("My name is Ree-knee. It is spelled like Ruh-nay but pronounced with two long *e*'s, Ree-knee.) Giving people a way to associate your name with you helps them remember you and your name.

Once you start talking, ask a lot of open-ended questions. (Who, what, when, where, how—notice I left out *why*—it is too judgmental.) For example, Have you been to one of these events? Do you know many people here? What do you enjoy most about this organization? Are you a member? Did you hear any good speakers or attend any special sessions? Most people love to talk about themselves if you give them a chance.

When it's your turn to talk, what do you say? I can guarantee that you will be asked one of two questions, so prepare your answers. The first question will come from someone you are meeting for the first time. He/she is bound to ask, "What do you do?" Since you know in advance this will be asked, prepare!

What do you do? Most people answer this question with a job, a company, or a position/title. In general, these are answers that lead nowhere and make a forgettable impression. Take my own example. When working at IBM, if someone asked me what I did, there were several ways I could have responded:

Forgettable: I am an engineer.

Equally forgettable: I work for IBM.

Even worse, as it is full of jargon: I am an engineer working in C4 interconnections and MLC packaging for IBM.

Better: I help the semiconductor chips in all your devices connect so your laptop, car, and games all work when you turn them on.

Best: I make the Sony Playstation, Xbox, and Wii work.

The last answer not only generated a lot of interest, but more importantly, people remembered it! (And asked me if I could get them a discount.)

Try It Now

What Do You Do?

What do you do? Make the answer as interesting as possible. Try it out on a few people and keep improving it as you get their reactions or as you take on new challenges.

The second question you will be asked will come from someone you know. He/she will most likely ask, "What's new?" or "How have you been?" The most common answers I hear are "Same old" or "Not much." Not really great conversation starters! You have a chance to be remembered, so give a memorable answer.

Think about what you have been working on lately, places you have recently visited or plan to visit, a class you might be taking, some positive life or professional event, or something coming up that you are excited about. As funny stories happen to you or you attend fun events, think about how to turn these into an interesting answer.

Try It Now

What's New?

What's new? Write your answer.

Now that you have an answer, test it.

- Does it encourage more questions?
- Is it positive?
- Is it a good icebreaker?

If the answers are yes, go with it. If not, start again, What's new?

If you know the person well enough to remember your last conversation, instead of asking them, "What's new?", ask them how they made out on the project they were working on, or whether they had taken any more interesting trips like the last one you discussed, or whatever connection you can make. This not only opens the conversation but also shows you remember them and were truly interested in them.

After the conversation has started, there may be some pauses as you finish a topic. If this makes you uncomfortable, the best solution is again to be prepared. Think about a few topics you are very familiar with and also some you would love to know more about. Just preparing this list in advance helps get you in a "networking frame of mind." You may never get to all or even some of the topics, but having prepared this can be very helpful if you are shy or have trouble thinking of things to say.

You might complain that this is really contrived and that you would rather be genuine and natural. If you are comfortable doing that, great.

However, I would also ask you, if you had to give a major presentation to a client or to a high-level executive, would you prepare ahead? Of course you would. Why is this any different?

The purpose of a networking event is to meet people. You want to circulate and meet as many people as you can, but you don't want to insult someone by cutting the conversation short. One of my ways to move along is to ask the people I am with if they'd like to get some food, drink, or hors d'oeuvres. If there is no food but some items are on display, you might ask if they want to go look at them. As you move on, it is easy to start conversations with others as you go.

You do need to assure that when you move on, you are not leaving the person you have been talking with stranded. This is easy to do in a group, but if you are speaking with just one person, you might look to introduce the person to someone else so that moving on is easier. Or you might invite the person to circulate with you. When you do part ways, always end with a thank-you and a follow-up line. Some examples:

- Would you mind if I contacted you to learn more?
- I need to speak to someone who just came in, but I would like to follow up on that contact you mentioned. Can I send you an e-mail and get his/her number?
- I'm going to circulate a bit, but thank you for explaining _____ to me. Can I contact you in the future if I have any questions?

The main point is to thank people, move on, and keep the path open for a follow-up or reconnection.

If you still have butterflies about meeting new people, get to the events early. It is much easier to approach someone when there are few people around than when you are trying to break into conversations already started or interrupt large crowds. I noticed this same behavior in my three-year-old granddaughter. When she arrives at preschool early and is one of the first children there, she runs right in and "owns" the classroom. But when she arrives a little bit later and the class is full, she is more tentative, more clingy, and a bit less certain.

What about business cards? When should you exchange them? There is no absolute time to exchange cards—some people like to do it when you first meet, others as you leave. In either case, *make sure you do* exchange cards. You may think you will never meet that person again, or you will remember his or her name, but you never know. Keep your cards separated from the ones you receive and try to keep the ones you receive in order so you can put names and faces together later.

More important than when you exchange cards is what you do with them. When you get home, do you throw them in a drawer? The very best thing to do is to go through them immediately after the event and write comments on the back about everyone you met—what they look like, what they do, what you discussed, and most importantly, how you might *follow up*.

I like to put all this information into a database that can be sorted while others like to keep the hardcopy cards. Either is fine as long as you can locate them before you attend another similar event or conference, and that you organize them for following-up.

When I began my career training and consulting business, the first place I started looking for contacts was my card file, and I prepared a note followed by a call to let them know "what was new." Some of the people I had not spoken to in several years (you cannot follow up regularly with everyone), so I reminded them of what we had done together when I called. The thing I found most surprising was that I got the best leads and connections from people I never expected would provide any, so keep all lines of communication open.

If you want to strengthen your ties to people, follow up. People are not going to call you unless you call them. If you left with a follow-up and a promise to do something, do it. This is the best reason to call, as you not only reconnect, but you also show that you deliver on what you promise.

If the reason to call isn't obvious, making the call can be a scary prospect. To help you get started, here are some "reasons" you might call:

- You have some new news you want to share (new position, new degree, life event, new company, etc.)
- The person mentioned something they were going to do and you wondered how he/she made out.

- You took the person's advice on something, and it worked, so you are calling to say thank you. (Always look for opportunities to say thank you!)
- The event you met at is coming up again, and you wondered if he/she was planning to attend. Or a similar one is happening, and you wondered if he/she knew about it.
- And, of course, there's the old standby: "I haven't heard from you in a long time and wondered what was new." (And make sure you have your own answer for what's new.)

When you do make that first call, remind the person where you met and what you talked about. You don't want them to waste time trying to remember who you are and thus not listening to what you are saying.

Try It Now
Reconnecting

Make a list of the people you want to reconnect with this month and how you want to connect (call, card, e-mail, etc.).

Now make the reconnection.

Repeat this at the start of every month.

If you practice and perfect the techniques in this chapter, you will unleash possibilities far beyond any you can imagine. None of them will occur if you stay in your cubicle, laboratory, or office. Reach out to your friends, to the friends of your friends, and ignite your networking chain reaction today.

10

WILL YOU BE MY MENTOR?

Many people have gone further than they thought they could because someone else thought they could.
—Unknown

Throughout this book I have given you advice about issues and opportunities that may arise throughout your career. However, no book can be customized to your specific needs or problems; and that is why every career woman should have a mentor, coach, or confidante to provide that personal support.

In my first fifteen years with IBM, I had no mentor. I do remember a very senior manager inviting me into his office somewhere between my fifth and tenth year telling me IBM was starting a mentoring program, and he was going to be my mentor. I asked him what that meant, and his response was, "I'm not sure, but I think it means if you have any questions or problems, come see me." Needless to say, I never went back.

Being a woman manager and executive, I was often sought out by other female engineers for advice, and as IBM formalized its mentoring processes and more importantly training of mentors and mentees, I found myself devoting several hours each week to helping other engineers, male and female, succeed. But I fell into a trap. Because I was helping so many others, I didn't think I really needed a mentor. As such, I would fill someone's name in on the blank for development plans but never really followed through. It wasn't until I was at a career crossroads that I even considered that I could use a mentor.

My first mentoring session happened because I actively sought it. I had an individual working for me who was going through some very difficult decisions in her career. While we spoke regularly about her concerns, I found that I was not being as objective as I could have been because her decisions affected my organization's work output. This individual had identified a mentor in corporate with a significant amount of experience in many areas of IBM. When my employee shared with me some of the advice her mentor had provided, it opened my eyes. This was excellent advice, given from a perspective I had never considered. It made me think, if mentoring can help my employee, why am I not taking advantage of it?

So I called the individual who was mentoring my employee and described my situation and career questions. She connected me to another individual who became one of my strongest advisors. My mentor forced me to reevaluate my goals and what I meant by success. She introduced me to opportunities I had no idea existed. She gave me the confidence to make a major career change that turned out to be a pivotal step in my becoming a distinguished engineer. And she connected me to technical resources within and outside the company upon whom I still rely for advice and expertise.

After the mentor I had been working with retired, I started a new relationship with someone whom I thought had the attributes and experience to help me with my next goals. Unfortunately, that relationship did not work as effectively, and after the second meeting, we agreed that our experiences were just too different to provide a common ground for mentoring. I then went on to find another mentor (and several since then).

I tell this story for several reasons. First, you may feel your career is going along just fine, that your manager is taking care of you, and that you are reaching your goals, so you don't need a mentor. The answer, which became obvious to me when I found the right mentor, was that it could have been going even better. Second, just having a mentor is meaningless if you don't work at it. Having a meeting for the sake of meeting accomplishes no more than the executive who told me to see him if I had any problems. Finally, not every mentoring relationship works. If it doesn't, end it.

Like anything else worthwhile, successful mentoring relationships require effort. In this chapter, I will describe steps you can take, as a mentor or mentee, to make sure your relationship is meaningful and meeting your needs.

What is a mentor anyway? A mentor is not a shoulder to cry on, nor is a mentee someone you want to turn into a clone of yourself. Mentor was the wise and faithful advisor to Odysseus in Greek mythology, and to me that is the key role a mentor plays—a personal advisor, one focused specifically on *you* and your needs. Mentors are also role models, sponsors, coaches, and connections to an even greater network. A mentor is not necessarily a friend, but may ultimately become one.

Women and minorities have special needs that make mentoring critical to their career growth. Natural networking opportunities may not exist, and their needs may not match those of their male counterparts. Most studies show that while candidates for fast tracks in business are frequently chosen from white males within their first few years, the minority and female candidates often take longer to be identified. Whether this is because women tend to downplay their accomplishments and not ask for more, or whether there are other factors at play, a good mentoring relationship will raise your awareness of this and others' awareness of you.

An example of this gender awareness and the help a mentor can provide happened within our location at IBM when we were looking to name people "master inventors." This prestigious honor is given each year to people who have made a significant contribution to intellectual property and patents, and is coordinated through a technical vitality council. Once a year, internal communications published an announcement that the selection process was beginning and included application forms. In the first year, we had only one woman apply. In the second year, we had none. In the third year, I personally got involved to query our patent database for the top inventors and found that more than 25 percent of the top inventors were women. Moreover, many had hundreds of significant inventions! I invited the top female inventors to a roundtable to ask why they did not apply. Some were unaware of the program, but the vast majority never thought their contributions were so unique that they were worthy! One woman who had over two-hundred inventions said she didn't realize she was competitive for this!

Tell me that women don't downplay their contributions. After a pep talk from me and other executives, many of these women did apply and were selected. If these women had technical mentors (which not one did), I am convinced they would have been encouraged to apply earlier. Thanks to this experience and management assistance, almost all have since found mentors.

Since mentoring is so important to your career, let's step back and review some mentoring basics to help you get started. How do you find a mentor? It starts by deciding what help you need.

Try It Now
Matchmaker, Matchmaker, Make Me a Match—How to Pick a Mentor

- Step 1—Answer these questions:

  1. What am I good at?
  2. What am I weak at?
  3. When have I said to myself, "if only I could be more like . . ."?
  4. What special needs or situations am I facing (e.g., work-life balance, diversity, difficulty speaking in large groups, etc.)?
  5. What is keeping me from attaining what I want?
  6. Do I want ongoing guidance, help with a specific problem, networking, or something else?

- Step 2

  1. Summarize these needs into the most important areas you want to address.
  2. Then start your search for the right person to help you solve them.

After completing this exercise, you know the traits you are looking for. I also like to add what I call the "ble's." Your mentor needs to be:

- Credible
- Available
- Responsible
- Admirable
- Capable
- Respectable
- Flexible
- Approachable

Your mentor should be a balance of what you have and what you lack. Let me explain. Working with a mentor who has similar experiences to yours provides a good starting point for sharing. However, you also want to choose someone who is good at what you may consider a shortcoming. For example, if you are a weak communicator, try to choose someone with excellent communication skills. You may want someone with more knowledge in an area of expertise. Or you may want to choose someone who knows how to handle themselves during tough or high-stress situations. You may want someone who has similar child care issues and has resolved them. The ideal mentor brings an expertise and experience base that you want to enhance while not being so far removed that you can't relate to each other. You need someone like you, but not so much like you that you limit your learning.

Similarly, when choosing a mentor, you want to consider the hierarchy gap between you and your mentor. I definitely believe your mentor should not be your immediate manager. In fact, I think it is better if your mentor is outside your management chain entirely. If he/she is within your chain, then the mentor should be at least a few levels above yours. A little distance helps assure objectivity on both sides. My most valuable mentoring relationships were with mentors outside my organization and a few levels above mine.

A special note for mentors. If you agree to be a mentor for someone else, should you be looking for the same traits? Not exactly. When I assess whether I can and should mentor an individual, I consider his or her "ent's."

- Commitment
- Talent

- Time well spent
- Desire for development and career advancement
- Accomplishment

And last but far from least:

- Potential

Being a mentor, while time-consuming, has tremendous payback both personally and for your company. When I was promoted to executive, I attended a training class where I was asked what I was doing to prepare the next generation of leaders to take my job. If you want your company to succeed, you need to develop new leaders, and you have a responsibility to mentor your successors. But it is a two-way street. You can learn a tremendous amount from your mentees. You create future allies, as your mentees may someday be promoted to positions even higher than you hold.

If you have agreed to be a mentor, remember that you are now making a commitment. Don't leave the mentee hanging, as a lack of response cannot only be disappointing but can make him or her (especially her) feel rejected. Do no harm.

Back to mentees. Once you have identified the traits you are looking for in a mentor, where do you find him or her? Talk to your manager. Talk to your middle management. Talk to your coworkers. Check internal mentoring Web sites and mentor networks. Watch people in meetings. If you are a new hire, see if there is someone who is an alumnus of the same college you attended. Join a networking group and observe the leaders. Check professional societies and organizations in your field, especially members from your company. Check external mentoring Web sites. (One is listed in the bibliography.) However, if you are not planning to change firms, I do encourage you to find your mentor within your company whenever possible.

Your mentor search takes time, so be patient. As you meet people who might become your mentor, you will have increased the number of people you know, even if you decide the relationship isn't right. Often talking to one person leads you to another who is the right mentor. The search process can be valuable to your career in and of itself.

Once you have chosen a mentor, how do you get started? It's as easy as ABC(DE):

Ask
Become acquainted
Communicate
Document
Evaluate

The first meeting is an important step in assuring you and your mentor click, so you need to come prepared. Schedule one hour so you are not rushed and prepare yourself. A good first meeting should be about getting to know each other and what you want to achieve from the mentoring. Be prepared to answer the comment, "Tell me about yourself." The following exercise will help make that first impression a positive one.

Try It Now

Preparing for Your First Mentoring Session

1. Prepare a *short* bio (not a detailed resume).

2. Review the reasons you chose the particular mentor from the matchmaking exercise and the top areas you want to address.

3. Rank the reasons to help define what you want to achieve from the sessions. Review these at the first meeting to see whether your mentor feels these are items he/she can assist you with.

4. Provide your contact number or e-mail, and ask your mentor what method he/she prefers.

After the meeting, how did you feel? Did you connect? It takes time to build trust and confidence, but you usually know after the first meeting if it is worth scheduling additional ones.

Keep the communication going by scheduling meetings regularly. Use a "dentist-office" mentality—make your next appointment when leaving the prior one and schedule them at regular intervals. (But don't wait six months, like the dentist—you should see your mentor more often in the beginning and at the very least quarterly.) If a situation arises where you need advice right away, schedule a session as soon as possible.

When your session is finished, document what you talked about, any actions you or the mentor planned to take, and anything else you want to remember. You may want to share this with your mentor, or your mentor may want to keep his or her own notes. Either is fine. But just as you would keep track of any follow-ups or action items with your job, do the same with your mentoring. Also, if you are the mentor, I suggest you do the same. The next exercise suggests things you might document.

Try It Now

Keeping Records of Your Mentoring Sessions

- When you have a business or technical problem, you define the problem, define the steps to fix it, define the schedule in which you will do it, and then check to see if what you did worked. All this is documented and shared with the people who are looking for your action plans and results. Mentoring should be treated the same way.

- After each session, you should generate a record of the meeting to include the following:

  1. What was discussed?
  2. What actions were agreed to?
  3. When will those actions occur?
  4. When will you get back together?

- Whether you create a form to do this or write yourself a note to file, this document formalizes the mentoring process. You should also create a list of topics you would like to discuss at future sessions. Pull out the list periodically, especially when you are having a tough time on something, and update it.

Some of the techniques I have described in other chapters, such as making sure your goals have SMARTS or justifying your next promotion, will often help you and your mentor see where you are lacking in experience or opportunities.

Since mentoring is individual, there is no one-size-fits-all rule for your mentor-mentee relationship. However, good relationships maintain confidentiality, focus on follow-ups, and ask questions that make you look at your career and your goals objectively.

You should periodically evaluate your mentoring relationship to see if it is still serving your needs.

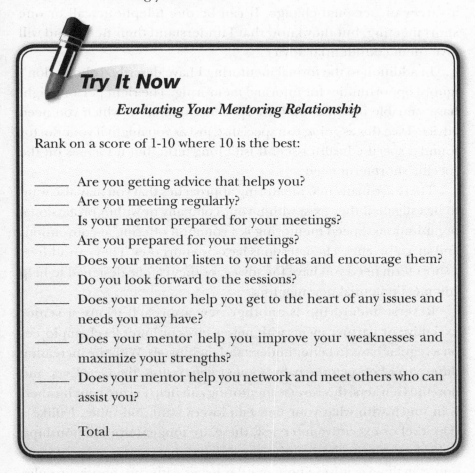

Try It Now

Evaluating Your Mentoring Relationship

Rank on a score of 1-10 where 10 is the best:

_____ Are you getting advice that helps you?
_____ Are you meeting regularly?
_____ Is your mentor prepared for your meetings?
_____ Are you prepared for your meetings?
_____ Does your mentor listen to your ideas and encourage them?
_____ Do you look forward to the sessions?
_____ Does your mentor help you get to the heart of any issues and needs you may have?
_____ Does your mentor help you improve your weaknesses and maximize your strengths?
_____ Does your mentor help you network and meet others who can assist you?

Total _____

Over time your score should improve, so don't worry if the score is low initially. However, if after several meetings you scored less than sixty-five, I would definitely reevaluate the relationship and how to improve it. If you feel you cannot improve it, or if you feel you have learned what you wanted to master from your mentor (the score will start dropping), it is time to move on. Similarly, a good mentor will tell you when you need to consider a new mentor because you need exposure or experience he/she cannot provide. This doesn't mean you have to sever the relationship completely, but you would meet less frequently and in a less-structured fashion (what I call informal mentoring). People I mentored ten years ago and who have moved into new areas often call me for advice about a career or personal change. It can be one telephone call or one short meeting, but they know that I understand their needs and will give them confidential advice.

In addition to the formal mentoring I have described above, don't ignore opportunities for informal mentoring. The right person might have valuable information for a specific situation in which you need advice. I see this as going to a specialist, just as you might if your doctor found a specific health issue. It isn't long-term, but it focuses on the specific short-term need.

There are many new mentoring approaches that you may also want to investigate if they exist within your company or within professional organizations. Speed mentoring is a common offering at conventions and special events. These sessions have two purposes. They can address a short-term need you have for advice, or they can be designed to help you meet potential new mentors.

Reverse mentoring is another new approach where a senior executive or partner meets with newer hires or lower-level employees on a regular basis to better understand their issues. With the increasing differences between the baby boomer generation, the Gen Xers, and now the Gen Yers, this reverse mentoring can help ensure your business is in touch with what your new employees want and value. Unlike a skip level or executive interview, these are longer-term relationships. In IBM, our women's executive network group reverse-mentored some senior male executives about gender issues with very positive results. Another special kind of mentoring is sponsoring an employee. This can occur when an executive puts the employee onto a staff or special assignment to help that employee increase his or her business awareness and network.

No matter what type of mentoring you choose, remember that the advice is only advice. What you ultimately decide to do is up to you. You own your life decisions, so take everyone's input and make the best decisions you can. Don't make my mistake and wait fifteen years to start. If you don't have a mentor, *get one*. If you don't have a mentee, *get one*. If you do have a mentor and a mentee, use the techniques in this chapter to kick the relationship up a notch. What are you waiting for? You own your career. Make it shine.

11

HAVING IT ALL

Life is a great big canvas; throw all the paint on it you can.
—Danny Kaye

After thirty-nine years of working in a man's world, raising children, and trying to "have it all," the most important message I can pass on is to know what makes you happy and go for it. So how do you decide if you have the right balance?

There is an exercise called a happiness wheel that I used many years ago, where I was asked to visualize my priorities as a pie with slices for career, money, family, health, social, and spiritual priorities. The instructor then asked us to rate each pie slice from 1 to 10 as to how satisfied we were with that particular slice. There was no right or wrong answer—you just decided where you were against where you wanted to be. The point of the exercise was to see if you were out of balance. If the wheel is uneven, it can't roll forward very well, and neither will you. For example, if your career satisfaction is a 9 but your family is a 5, you are probably putting too much emphasis on your career. If you are about the same in all areas (which doesn't mean devoting equal time to all areas—it's based on where you want to be, not some arbitrary standard), then you are probably doing the right things for your happiness. If you are out of whack in a few areas, think about what it takes to bring them back into balance and take a tiny step toward changing it. (Yes, a tiny step—because after the first, the rest get easier.) This is also a good exercise to do with your mentor.

By the way, the slices in this pie do not have to be just the six I listed above. You can make the wheel as large or as small as you want. Do you want to add a section for education, for pleasure and personal time, for financial goals, for artistic pursuits? It's up to you to include the items you think you want for your balance and then analyze your position against them.

Managing your priorities is important, but you should revisit this wheel periodically, as what makes you happy and what is important to you will change over time. When your children are small, when you are branching out into some major new area in your career, when your family needs you, when you have some unexpected expenditures, or whatever life brings, you will change your priorities and where you view yourself on the wheel. You are responsible for your happiness. Enjoy the trip as well as the destination. In fact, sometimes the trip is more fun. Turn your passions and strengths into success, whatever success means to you. You are responsible for how you feel. Act like it.

It is also important to give back as you advance your career. Others starting out need to learn from your experience, and women need to help other women succeed. Be yourself. Mentor and advise. This is more than just doing your job and becomes more important as you move up in your career.

Don't be too self-critical or hesitant to try new things. Not going for something because you are afraid to fail is a very female behavior that will impede your career. I had a mentor who would ask me in stages, "What's the worst that can happen?" If I would say, "I don't think I should . . . ," my mentor would ask, "What's the worst that can happen?" I'd answer, "I might not be able to do it." My mentor would again ask, "What's the worst that can happen?" Through this process I came to realize the outcome of taking the risk, and failing was often exactly the same as if I never tried! I had nothing to lose by trying something new.

Try It Now
What's the Worst that Can Happen?

- When you are hesitant about taking on something new, there are many pep talks you can have with yourself or with your mentor. Use this worksheet to help you decide how to move forward.

  1. State the concern or opportunity and what you could do about it.

     Now imagine the worst that can happen. What would that be?

     What would be the result to you if the worst happened?

     What would the result of doing nothing be?

- In many cases, you will find that the result of doing nothing or not taking on the challenge is exactly the same as trying and failing. So what do you really have to lose?

  2. To make yourself even more confident consider the following:

     What can I do to make sure the worst doesn't happen?

     What would I do if the worst did happen?

Do not obsess over mistakes. You will make mistakes, and you will learn more from them than your successes. Good judgment comes from experience, and experience comes from bad judgment! Successful people fail much more often than unsuccessful people. Mickey Mantle had the most strikeouts of any baseball player. (See, I even used a sports analogy; that comes from working in a man's world.) In fact, you probably should make more mistakes because that means you are stretching yourself. What and how you learn from these experiences is what makes the difference. Learn to forgive yourself. Most women forgive others much more quickly than themselves.

Perfection doesn't exist; it's an ideal, not a reality. Women worry too much about being perfect when they are already good enough. You can't have a rainbow without rain, so don't take the setbacks personally. You can be whatever you truly want. You are intelligent. Believe in yourself. You deserve your right to shine. Instead of telling yourself you can't or what you ought to do, ask yourself, "What if?" or "How about?" These questions are much more mind opening.

Throughout your career, you will move through new challenges and have opportunities to take on new roles, be it in the same area or a completely different one. Your decision to move or stay put may be related to where you are on your S curve.

S curves are a scientific description of how bacterial colonies multipy but they also describe the process of learning and growing. When you start something new, you are at your maximum learning rate but contributing little. As you climb the curve, you start to contribute more. At the peak of the curve, you are of most value to your company as you are contributing fully and know your stuff. The problem is, over time you can get stale, and your productivity decreases. While you may be feeling very competent and comfortable in your assignment, that very sense of ease can hold you back. At this point, you need a new assignment or a new project or even a new position to move you back up the curve and even higher than before! An S curve looks like this over time:

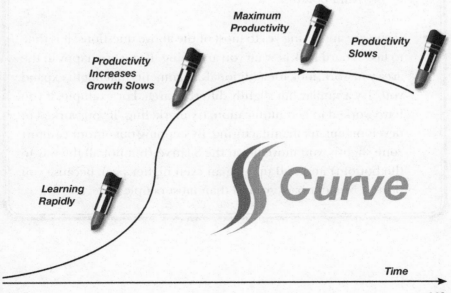

So where are you on your S curve?

Try It Now

Where Are You on Your S Curve?

- How do you recognize when you have peaked and are slowing? Ask yourself these questions.

    1. Am I saying to myself, "Here we go again"?

    2. Am I telling others, "That won't work because we tried it before"?

    3. What new tasks have I done in the last month, and did I learn anything new from them?

    4. Am I excited about this new assignment?

    5. Am I challenged and seeking advice, or do I know exactly how to do what is needed?

    6. Am I bored?

- If you are answering yes to most of the above questions, it is time to take a hard look at what you are doing. If you are happy in the area you work, look for additional assignments that might expand you. Try a similar but slightly different area. For example, if you have worked in communication, try marketing. If you worked in development, try manufacturing. By stepping out of your comfort zone slightly, you move down the S curve (but not all the way to the bottom) and end up with an even higher peak because you bring a broader background than most people have.

So is it time for a change? Are you out of balance? Are you at a crossroads in your career? What should you do next? What if you . . . ? How about . . . ? What are you looking for in your next assignment? Money, more flexible hours, advancement, challenge, growth? What is your gut reaction to this opportunity? If you find your gut is positive or negative, it is usually right. Don't wait for opportunity to knock; shop around periodically.

The world is always changing. Opportunities for success abound, but they may be different from the ones to which you have become accustomed. Try something new and enjoy the learning. You are responsible for your happiness—grab it. Possibility is just one step away.

12

BEHIND EVERY SUCCESSFUL WOMAN IS A GOOD MAN

Few things in the world are more powerful than a positive push.

—*Richard M. DeVos*

Much of this book has been directed at female employees to encourage them to use all their potential. However, as a man working with women, as a male manager of women, as a company executive trying to maximize your resources, or as a man working for a woman, there are some specific items you must consider to make your work environment the most productive it can be. Companies need to attract, develop, and retain the best people for the job, regardless of gender or ethnicity. It is, frankly, good business.

Women often find that the mid point in their career is a critical time for advancement. If managers are insensitive to the barriers they erect, women may leave their organization at a point when their exit is most costly. This high cost of turnover is avoidable if you make a conscious effort to change your culture.

The first step is realizing that there is a difference, and the very techniques that make you a good coach for men may not apply to women. I have a friend who went from coaching his son's Little League team to coaching his daughter's. He had started with both at the age of seven. He lamented to me that the first day of practice with the girls, he had to get used to the fact that the girls in the outfield often practiced cartwheels when the game got slow. He had to completely change his methods to bring out the best in his all-female team. He did more explaining, let the girls ask a lot of questions, asked them what positions they wanted to play, complimented them often, and listened. He also carefully explained that it was difficult to catch a ball when you were upside down. As a result, his team had a very successful season. Your female employees may have their own version of cartwheels in the outfield that you need to understand and tolerate.

What should you do if you are managing very capable women to help bring out their best? Whether you are a male or female boss, manager, or leader, be aware of the differences. Help force goal setting. Send your employees to classes to let them try new experiences. Let them shadow someone at a higher level. Ask yourself if you are holding them back because they aren't pushing you. Check on their projects to be sure they are not waiting until they are "perfect" to bring them forward. Help build their self-confidence in their achievements, as success breeds more success.

Whether your company is delivering products or services, remember that half of consumers are women (and in general make most of the buying decisions in a family). They will bring issues and solutions men might not even think about. A good example was the Ford Windstar minivan, which was introduced in the 1990s and was a major success at that time. One fourth of the design team for this minivan was female. They added features like a backup alert system, a low-wattage dome light so it didn't glare in a baby's face, bins for diapers, and other items designed for a family's needs. Windstar's market share climbed after these items were introduced. Volvo had a similar experience. Be it the iPod, the space program, global warming, health care, or whatever business you are in, varying points of view, including gender input, bring a balanced perspective to your technical, business, marketing, or sales team that you can directly turn into profits. Since developing and retaining women is smart business, learn to excel at it.

As a manager or coworker, always be open and forthcoming. Women deserve the same honesty that you would give a man. I have seen managers afraid to provide constructive criticism to women because they do not want to upset them. Women can take criticism if it is done in a civilized fashion, and they believe you are working to help them improve. This means having some specific suggestions of what they can do as opposed to generalities, and it also means that you have established a trusting relationship. Finally, these discussions should always be done in private. Women do not respond well to public appraisals (positive or negative). Men may like to be praised in public, but women tend to prefer to receive that recognition more privately so as not to be singled out. Moreover, what you say will affect a woman's behavior much longer than it will a man's. A woman will generally not respond to intimidation—she will often shut down or start looking elsewhere rather than strive harder.

Be aware of the differences in speech and expectations discussed in Chapter 2. Women will listen to what you say *and* to how you say it. Your body language is critical. Women respond to subtle body language signals much more quickly than men. So if you are giving praise but not showing that same enthusiasm in your mannerisms, they will not hear it the way you intended. Do the praising because they won't do it themselves, but do it in private for the person, in public for the team.

Marie von Ebner-Escenbach once stated, "Women are so vain they even care about the opinions of people they don't care for." I am not sure if it is vanity or lack of self-confidence, but women do take others' opinions to heart, regardless of where they come from. I recently spent an afternoon with two women who were discussing a particularly difficult male boss. One of the women stated she never thought he liked her. The second woman not only agreed with her, but stated that she had actually heard the male say this. Now, the first woman no longer worked for the individual, had long since written him off as someone whose opinion she did not value, and was a success in her own right. Yet when she heard confirmation of what she had thought, she was visibly upset. She still cared about the opinion of someone she didn't respect! Remember as you are bringing forward constructive criticism to keep it impersonal.

I observed a similar example of this with a recent mentee. She had always been rated as a top performer, but in the most recent year's rating she had dropped to an above-average rating. Her manager mentioned some specific areas in which she could improve to get her top rating back, most related to teamwork. She had been working sixty-hour weeks, had been a top technical performer, and was visibly hurt by the rating. She was questioning why she was working so hard and was ready to change jobs or move on. In contrast, at the same time I had been working closely with a male executive who received a very low rating because of the business performance of his unit, even though much of the reason for the business environment change was outside of his control. His reaction to the rating was, "They are wrong, and I am going to show them so next year I am a top performer again." He did not take it personally; he took it as a challenge. I used this example with my female mentee, helped her work through the personal issues, and helped her get to the heart of the problem. Once she accepted the challenge, she was ready to go out and "show them" herself. However, if we had not spoken, I believe she would have been so hurt by the rating change that she would have left the area and perhaps the business. Considering that she was an outstanding technical resource who gave much more than 100 percent to the job and could easily overcome the issues her manager had raised, that would have caused the business to be severely impacted. Had her manager done a better job of understanding how she would react and had he explained the issues while challenging her to "prove him wrong," she might not have taken it so personally.

It is also important to challenge women to reach for greater heights. Women often do not believe they can reach as high as a comparable male. Convince them they can and not to settle for something less. If you are mentoring women, pay close attention to this. As a manager, make sure to keep your female employees aware of opportunities and don't judge for yourself whether they would want it.

I recently got into a discussion with a coworker who has always practiced excellent people management and what I thought was excellent development of technical women. However, we were discussing his family, and he told me that he and his wife were encouraging his high school daughter to become a teacher. When I asked him why, he replied that they both felt teaching was an excellent career choice since it would provide her with flexibility in raising a family. I asked about her grades, and he indicated his daughter was a top student. Then I asked this high-level manager if he had any sons. He replied, "Yes, I have a son just entering college. He is going to major in engineering."

"That's interesting," I said. "So he must be better in science and math than your daughter."

"Actually," the father replied, "my daughter was a much better student than her brother in every subject."

"So you want your top-performing daughter to be a teacher and your less-than-top-performing son to be an engineer?" I asked. "What if your son were female? Would you want him to teach? And if your daughter were male, would you be directing her toward a different career?"

This senior manager looked at me for a few minutes, then turned red. He exclaimed, "Here I am thinking I am equitable in everything I do at IBM, and I have not been bringing that thinking home. Maybe I should have another talk with my daughter."

Now I am in no way, shape, or form stating that a teacher is not a respected or admirable profession; but as a parent, manager, or mentor, men (and women) can still fall into the trap of putting their own gender biases into their everyday life.

So I have to ask every male who is looking to get the best out of his female employees or coworkers: Are you consciously or unconsciously applying your biases? Are you giving women the same promotional and line-management opportunities as males, or are you holding back because you think you are giving them "balance"?

Women with families need to know you are behind them in terms of work-life balance. However, only they can determine what that is, so don't put your biases or opinions onto this. Have a straight talk with your female employees on what will help them best succeed at home and at work. I had a friend who left one company not because she wanted to leave but because she needed a more flexible schedule, which her current employer would not accommodate. She took a drop in pay to do this. She worked an almost identical job in the second company, brought in a significant amount of new business, and was extremely happy to have made the change.

Another positive step a male manager can take for his female employees is to recognize that their work-life balance situation may enable them to be much more efficient working from home. For example, if a working mother has a thirty-minute commute to work and must drop off or pick up for child care, car pooling, or some other time-specific pre- or post-work activity, allowing her to work from home may actually make her more effective. The extra time that would have been spent commuting is almost always spent instead on work, giving her nearly an extra hour a day. Using face time as a criterion for getting ahead works against females and the entire company. Look for ways to provide females with flexibility. Remember, women won't ask for help or special treatment, and they will leave rather than fail.

If your company already has women in leadership positions, congratulations. Now, ask yourself if you're getting the most from them. Are they mentoring other women to achieve? Are you encouraging them to do so? Positive female role models are one of the most positive steps a company can provide, so do whatever you can to support and enable women leaders to do this. Success breeds success.

Traditionally, companies have set their "average-age clocks" to correspond to a more typical male role. For example, in many companies potential executives or key technical leaders are often targeted early and assigned some very big visible project in their first ten years. This is right around the time many females are starting their families or doing considerable work-life balancing. Many years later, when the children are in school full-time and the females are free to devote more time to that big, highly visible assignment, they have already been passed over. Companies need to take this into account and perhaps reset the age clock for females to take better advantage of this. Many recent books describe women "opting out" of the workforce to become full-time mothers. I believe many of these cases occur because the company policies or managers were too inflexible. That is also why many working mothers choose to leave to start their own companies or pursue alternative careers.

Women are extremely successful entrepreneurs in their own small companies. What does this career choice offer that a larger firm cannot? The biggest one is flexibility. They also get immediate objective feedback based on how the marketplace responds to their product and their business results. If you want to retain these entrepreneurial women in your firm, you have to offer a similar environment.

Give women financial responsibility. Give them important line-management roles. Be prepared to move them in and out of these roles as their life balance changes. Get rid of the stereotypes. Remember, women aren't comfortable negotiating for what they want, so it is important to have your antenna up. Ask, never assume.

Finally, if you intend to market or sell your products to women, then you are clearly limiting your opportunities if you do not include women in your marketing initiatives. Women and men have different buying behaviors, and understanding the differences can help you better match your clients with your sales force, as well as enhance everyone's skill.

The future workforce will be more diverse in gender, age, and ethnicity. It will be a global enterprise and managers/leaders must adapt their behaviors and leadership styles to bring the changes this future "flat" world will require. Senior leaders set the tone, and your approach will be critical to successful competition. Be a champion for bringing the best people forward. Developing and retaining the best people will bring the best results—for the business and for you. Remember, results matter.

Bibliography

Babcock, Linda, and Sara Laschever. *Women Don't Ask, Negotiation and the Gender Divide*. NJ: Princeton University Press, 2003.

Baber, Anne, and Lynne Waymon. *Make Your Contacts Count: Know-How for Business and Career Success*. AMACOM, 2007.

Clutterback, David. *Everyone Needs a Mentor: Fostering Talent in Your Organization*, 4th ed. 2004.

Darmoni, Regina. *Real Mentors Tell You This*. Xlibris, 2007.

Difalco, Marcelle, and Jocelyn Herz. *The Big Sister's Guide to the World of Work*. Simon and Schuster, 2005.

Fisher, Donna. *Professional Networking for Dummies*. John Wiley and Sons, 2001.

Gray, John. *Men Are from Mars, Women Are from Venus*. NJ: HarperCollins Press, 1992.

Harvard Business School Press. *Coaching and Mentoring, How to Develop Top Talent and Achieve Stronger Performance*. HBS Publishing, 2004.

Heim, Pat. *The Power-Dead Even Rule and Other Gender Differences in the Workplace*. Video from the Heim Group.

Patterson, Kerry, Joseph Grenny, Ron McMillan, and Al Switzler. *Crucial Confrontations*. NJ: McGraw Hill Publishing, 2005.

Stutz, Elinor. *Nice Girls Get the Sale.* Sourcebooks, 2006.

Whitmore, Sir John. *Coaching for Performance.* Nicholas Brealy Publishing, 2003.

Useful Web Sites:

http://entrepreneurs.about.com/od/businessnetworking/Business_Networking_for_Entrepreneurs.htm

http://www.businessknowhow.com/tips/networking.htm

http://www.pivotalcoaching.com/personal_coaching.php?thePage=pc_wheel.htm
http://www.topachievement.com/smart.html

http://sarah.lodick.com/edit/edit7550/task2.html

http://www.tipsforsuccess.org/difficult-people.htm

http://humanresources.about.com/od/workrelationships/a/difficultpeople.htm

http://www.itstime.com/mar99.htm

http://www.winning-at-work.net

http://www.mentors.ca/findamentor.html

For speaking engagements, contact *winningatwork@gmail.com.*

For more information visit *www.winning-at-work.net*